FitnessGram®
Administration Manual

The Journey to MyHealthyZone™

FIFTH EDITION

The Cooper Institute

HUMAN KINETICS

Library of Congress Cataloging-in-Publication Data

Names: Cooper Institute (Dallas, Tex.), issuing body.
Title: FitnessGram administration manual : the journey to MyHealthyZone / The
  Cooper Institute.
Other titles: FitnessGram/ActivityGram.
Description: Fifth edition. | Champaign, IL : Human Kinetics, 2017. | Revised
  edition of: FitnessGram/ActivityGram. Updated Fourth Edition. 2010. |
  Includes bibliographical references.
Identifiers: LCCN 2016015813| ISBN 9781450470469 (print) | ISBN 9781492508465
  (e-book)
Subjects: LCSH: Physical fitness for children--Testing. | Physical education
  and training--Study and teaching.
Classification: LCC GV436.5 .F58 2017 | DDC 372.86--dc23 LC record available at https://lccn.loc.gov/2016015813

ISBN: 978-1-4504-7046-9 (print)

This book is a revised edition of *FITNESSGRAM/ACTIVITYGRAM Test Administration Manual, Updated Fourth Edition,* published in 2010 by The Cooper Institute.

The web addresses cited in this text were current as of September 2016, unless otherwise noted.

Acquisitions Editors: Scott Wikgren and Kathy Read; **Developmental Editor:** Ragen E. Sanner; **Managing Editor:** Derek Campbell; **Copyeditor:** Tom Tiller; **Permissions Manager:** Dalene Reeder; **Senior Graphic Designer:** Joe Buck; **Cover Designer:** The Cooper Institute; **Photograph (cover):** Photo by Nichole C Stephens (nicholestephens.com); **Photographer (interior):** Neil Bernstein; photographs © Human Kinetics, unless otherwise noted; photos in chapter 7 © The Cooper Institute; **Photo Asset Manager:** Laura Fitch; **Visual Production Assistant:** Joyce Brumfield; **Photo Production Manager:** Jason Allen; **Senior Art Manager:** Kelly Hendren; **Illustrations:** © Human Kinetics, unless otherwise noted; **Printer:** Versa Press

We thank Pantego Christian Academy in Arlington, Texas and Thomas C. Marsh Middle School in Dallas, Texas for assistance in providing the location for the photo and video shoot for this book.

The video contents of this product are licensed for educational public performance for viewing by a traditional (live) audience, via closed circuit television, or via computerized local area networks within a single building or geographically unified campus. To request a license to broadcast these contents to a wider audience—for example, throughout a school district or state, or on a television station—please contact your sales representative (www.HumanKinetics.com/SalesRepresentatives).

Printed in the United States of America   10 9 8 7 6 5 4

The paper in this book is certified under a sustainable forestry program.

Human Kinetics
P.O. Box 5076
Champaign, IL 61825-5076
Website: www.HumanKinetics.com

In the United States, email info@hkusa.com or call 800-747-4457.
In Canada, email info@hkcanada.com.
In the United Kingdom/Europe, email hk@hkeurope.com.

For information about Human Kinetics' coverage in other areas of the world,
please visit our website: **www.HumanKinetics.com**

E6203

Contents

Part III ActivityGram Assessment Module 103

Manual Quick Guide

This manual provides fundamental information about FitnessGram and its role in a complete physical education or physical activity program. The manual is divided into three parts:

- Part I provides background information, including testing guidelines and appropriate uses.
- Part II provides FitnessGram test administration protocols and addresses how to administer each test and interpret the results.
- Part III addresses administration of Activity-Gram and ActivityGram Lite (Youth Activity Profile); it also provides guidelines for interpreting the physical activity results.

Throughout this manual, the features in the Key to Icons sidebar provide additional information about incorporating FitnessGram, ActivityGram, ActivityGram Lite, and ActivityLog into a physical education program.

This edition of the manual includes an accompanying web resource, which you can access by using the following URL: www.HumanKinetics.com/FitnessGramAdministrationManual. If you purchased a new print book, the directions for accessing the web resource are included on the orange-framed page at the front of this book. If you purchased an e-book from HumanKinetics.com, directions for accessing the web resource appear before the title page. The web resource includes video clips for all test protocols, music cadences for certain tests (e.g., PACER), and PDF files of forms and charts. The test protocol video clips demonstrate the proper way to implement each test and can also be used to teach proper technique to students.

Key to Icons

 Spotlight features provide real-world testimonials from avid users.

 How to Apply features relate content to best instructional practices.

 Key Concepts features emphasize main ideas at the end of each chapter.

 Web resource icons appear in the text to indicate video, reproducible, and cadence materials available in the web resource.

Acknowledgments

Appreciation is extended to the following people who serve on the FitnessGram Scientific Advisory Board; they have contributed many dedicated hours to the continued development and refinement of the program.

Joey C. Eisenmann, PhD, Michigan State University

Scott B. Going, PhD, University of Arizona

Dolly D. Lambdin, PhD, University of Texas at Austin

Matthew T. Mahar, EdD, East Carolina University

James R. Morrow, Jr., PhD, University of North Texas

Sharon A. Plowman, PhD, Northern Illinois University, retired

Stephen J. Pont, MD, MPH, FAAP, Dell Children's Medical Center

Georgi Roberts, MS, Fort Worth Independent School District, Texas

Gregory J. Welk, PhD, Iowa State University, Scientific Director

Weimo Zhu, PhD, University of Illinois at Urbana-Champaign

Emeritus Members

Steven N. Blair, PED, MPH, University of South Carolina

Charles B. Corbin, PhD, Arizona State University, retired

Kirk J. Cureton, PhD, University of Georgia, retired

Harold B. Falls, Jr., PhD, Southwest Missouri State University

Baker C. Harrell, PhD, Active Life, Inc.

Harold W. Kohl, PhD, University of Texas

Timothy G. Lohman, PhD, University of Arizona

Marilu D. Meredith, EdD, The Cooper Institute, former FitnessGram Program Director

Robert P. Pangrazi, PhD, Arizona State University, retired

Russell R. Pate, PhD, University of South Carolina

Judith J. Prochaska, PhD, MPH, University of California at San Francisco

Sara Jane Quinn, Baltimore County Public Schools, retired

Margaret J. Safrit, PhD, American University

James F. Sallis, PhD, San Diego State University

Charles L. Sterling, EdD, The Cooper Institute, Founder

Primary Writers

Marilu Meredith, EdD, The Cooper Institute, former FitnessGram Program Director

Gregory J. Welk, PhD, Iowa State University, Scientific Director

Contributing Writers

Kelly Allums-Featherston, PhD

Katelin Anderson, MS, The Cooper Institute

Norma Candelaria, MS, The Cooper Institute

Don Disney, MA, MS

Brian Mosier, PhD, University of Western Georgia

Catherine Vowell, MBA

Introduction

The field of physical education has seen many developments in the last few years. One key development was the publication in 2012 of a report titled *Fitness Measures and Health Outcomes in Youth,* which was produced by the Institute of Medicine (IOM) at the request of the Robert Wood Johnson Foundation. (The report defines youth as children aged 5 to 18 years.) Specifically, the report was put together by an IOM study committee appointed to assess the relationship between youth fitness test items and health outcomes, recommend the best fitness test items, provide guidance for interpreting fitness scores, and provide an agenda for needed research. In 2013, the report was reviewed by The Cooper Institute's FitnessGram Scientific Advisory Board, which outlined an action plan to address the IOM recommendations, including changes to enhance FitnessGram.

One change that software users will find helpful in FitnessGram and ActivityGram is that all of The Cooper Institute's tests and programs can now be accessed through a common dashboard called MyHealthyZone. This new name recognizes The Cooper Institute's emphasis on the fact that overall health involves not only fitness, and not only activity, but a combination of many factors, including fitness, activity, and sport. The MyHealthyZone dashboard is personalized for each administrator, teacher, student, or parent user. In addition to assessment events and results, MyHealthyZone features new data management and analysis tools, new reports, and SmartCoach (a content library providing user-specific information and materials about physical fitness and physical activity).

This manual describes how to implement and use data gathered through the FitnessGram test protocol; it also addresses how to use ActivityGram and ActivityGram Lite to help students achieve overall fitness and activity goals that benefit their health for a lifetime. The manual does not, however, remind users about MyHealthyZone, because software users will use it automatically through the new dashboard. If you have previously used the software, you need only update to the new version or purchase a license for the FitnessGram software. Once that has been accomplished, you will receive your login informa-

tion, after which you can visit https://myhealthy zone.fitnessgram.net and get started.

When you log in, MyHealthyZone recognizes you as either an administrator, a teacher, a student, or a parent and then begins to personalize your dashboard. The dashboard adds more personalization and suggests resources as you continue to interact with the software. Instructors who do not have the software can still use aspects of FitnessGram and ActivityGram in the form of reproducible forms and charts available in the accompanying web resource. However, doing so without the MyHealthyZone dashboard greatly limits one's experience with FitnessGram and ActivityGram.

In 2012, a group of five U.S. nonprofit groups and government agencies formed a national partnership to help schools use FitnessGram to assess students, support teachers through staff development, and begin providing incentives and awards to students by 2018. To pursue this goal, the partnership created the Presidential Youth Fitness Program, better known as the PYFP, which replaced the President's Youth Fitness Test. The partnership was formed by the following groups: The Cooper Institute; the U.S. Centers for Disease Control and Prevention; the President's Council on Fitness, Sports, and Nutrition; the Society of Health and Physical Educators (SHAPE America); and the National Foundation on Fitness, Sports, and Nutrition.

Another contribution to the field has been made by the NFL PLAY 60 campaign. In this program, the NFL Foundation (the charitable foundation of the National Football League) partners with other organizations to address childhood obesity by encouraging youth to be physically active for at least 60 minutes per day. For example, the NFL has partnered with the National Dairy Council to create the Fuel Up to Play 60 in-school program that encourages youth to engage in physical activity and eat a healthy diet. The two groups also founded the GENYOUth Foundation, which, along with the American College of Sports Medicine and the American School Health Association, released the Wellness Impact Report in 2013. The report addresses the importance of physical activity and good nutrition in positioning students to learn. In addition, as part of a partnership between NFL PLAY 60 and The Cooper Institute, the FitnessGram assessment is being implemented in schools throughout the 32 communities that are home to NFL franchises. The assessment is part of a longitudinal study that tracks health-related fitness results and analyzes how best to intervene. The results of the study will be provided to local, state, and national policy makers.

FitnessGram has been used as the gold-standard metric for youth fitness in research studies over the past 20 years. The most cited of all studies is the Texas Youth Fitness Study, which was conducted in 2009 in partnership with three universities, as well as The Cooper Institute and the Robert Wood Johnson Foundation. The study explored three key questions:

- Is physical fitness associated with academic performance?
- Can physical education teachers collect high-quality information about student fitness?
- Are school policies and environments associated with youth fitness?

A summary of the study is available from the Robert Wood Johnson Foundation (2011).

Collectively, these developments provide physical educators and youth-fitness promoters with considerable support and with guidelines for promoting physical activity and fitness in children. FitnessGram keeps pace with such developments and therefore keeps you on the cutting edge of promoting youth fitness.

PART I

Introduction to FitnessGram and ActivityGram

FitnessGram was created in 1982 by The Cooper Institute to provide an easy way for physical education teachers to report information to parents about their children's fitness levels. As was the case then, today's students are assessed in the following areas of health-related fitness: aerobic capacity, muscular strength, muscular endurance, flexibility, and body composition. Scores are evaluated against objective, criterion-referenced standards—referred to as Healthy Fitness Zone standards—that indicate the level of fitness necessary for health.

The FitnessGram software generates personalized reports that provide objective feedback and positive reinforcement; these reports serve as a communication link between teachers, students, and parents. Teachers without access to FitnessGram software can still use the FitnessGram assessment and can use the online FitnessGram calculator to determine and track scores for their classes; however, any individual feedback and activity suggestions would be developed by the teacher. The FitnessGram individual reports provide feedback based on whether a given child achieved the criterion-referenced standards for physical activity or fitness; the reports also foster students' ability to read and interpret results and to set goals. In addition, the use of health-related criteria helps minimize comparisons between children and emphasizes personal fitness for health rather than goals based on performance. Beyond the individual benefits, aggregate reporting allows administrators to view de-identified summary data for an entire campus, district, or state. Aggregate reporting also provides surveillance data that allow educators to identify trends that can inform curricular and programmatic decisions.

The following list describes the modules found in the FitnessGram application that can be used to highlight the importance of fitness and physical activity:

- FitnessGram includes a complete battery of health-related fitness items scored according to criterion-referenced standards. These standards are age- and sex-specific and are established based on how fit children need to be for the purpose of good health.

- ActivityGram provides detailed information about a student's level of physical activity; specifically, it provides feedback about both the amount and the type of activity that a child performs. Teachers can use either a three-day recall assessment or a brief survey.

- ActivityLog allows students to track their physical activity in terms of either a step count or minutes of activity per day. Teachers can use this tool to issue challenges to students, classes, and schools to increase their physical activity.

- SmartCoach, the new content library, is packed with staff development resources, communication materials, instructional materials, and resources for educating students and parents.

These diverse components and features of FitnessGram help teachers and students establish healthy habits for a lifetime.

Part I of this manual addresses the mission and philosophy of the FitnessGram program (chapter 1), principles of fitness education and assessment guidelines in physical education (chapter 2), guidelines for promoting physical activity in children (chapter 3), and strategies for communicating with stakeholders (chapter 4).

Additional Resources

For information about the validity and reliability of the tests, as well as the rationale for the standards, teachers and administrators can consult the *FitnessGram/ActivityGram Reference Guide* (Plowman and Meredith 2013). Presented in a question-and-answer format, the guide addresses specific questions about the use and interpretation of FitnessGram and ActivityGram assessments. The guide may also be of interest to some parents who want more information about fitness. The guide can be accessed at the FitnessGram website; simply go to www.cooperinstitute.org/reference-guide.

Mission, Goals, and Philosophy of the FitnessGram Program

The FitnessGram program endorses a long-term view of physical education with the primary goal of promoting lifelong habits of physical activity. To be sure, physical education should also help individuals develop their fitness and improve their skills, but these objectives should be framed within the broader goal of helping students develop the knowledge, attitudes, and skills to be active for a lifetime.

The more specific goals of the FitnessGram program are to promote enjoyable, regular physical activity and to provide comprehensive physical fitness and activity assessments and reporting programs for children and youth. The program seeks to help individuals develop affective, cognitive, and behavioral components related to participation in regular physical activity regardless of sex, age, disability, or any other factor. Regular physical activity contributes to good health, the ability to function well in daily activities, and well-being; furthermore, in all of these ways, it remains important throughout a person's lifetime. Achievement of these goals can be facilitated by use of the FitnessGram program as part of a high-quality physical education program.

Like most of the U.S. population of all ages, children and youth have generally grown accustomed to a sedentary lifestyle. Indeed, an accelerometer study showed that 42 percent of children and only 8 percent of adolescents in the United States meet the Physical Activity Guidelines for Americans 2008 recommendation of at least 60 minutes of moderate to vigorous physical activity per day (Troiano et al. 2008). Thus it may not be surprising that children and youth face growing health risks, including increased obesity; in addition, we know that risks in a child can jeopardize her or his well-being as an adult. In this context, FitnessGram, as an assessment and report, is intended to create awareness and start a conversation about promoting a healthy lifestyle and increased physical activity. FitnessGram is, of course, just one part of the overall solution, which also includes instruction about fitness concepts and physical activity, student participation in activity, goal setting and planning personal fitness programs, and promoting and tracking physical activity, that will empower students to engage in healthy behaviors, but it is a significant part.

FITNESSGRAM

FitnessGram is a comprehensive fitness-assessment battery for youth. It includes a variety of health-related physical fitness tests designed to assess aerobic capacity, muscular strength, muscular endurance, flexibility, and body composition. For each of the health-related fitness components, criterion-referenced standards associated with good health have been established for children and youth.

FitnessGram software generates individual report cards summarizing each child's performance on each component of health-related fitness. These reports can be used by students, teachers, and parents. Students can use them in planning their personal fitness programs; teachers can use them in determining student needs and guiding students in their program planning; and parents can use them to gain understanding of their child's needs and to help the child participate in physical activity. The software also uses a comprehensive database to track fitness records over time, thus helping educators document and organize information about student outcomes; in fact, detailed reporting tools can be used to summarize class, school, and district outcomes.

ACTIVITYGRAM

ActivityGram, which is incorporated into the FitnessGram software, provides a detailed assessment of physical activity. This module includes two assessments: a three-day recall of physical activity and a short survey about physical activity. These assessments provide students with personalized information about their general level of physical activity and help them learn strategies for being physically active, both in and outside of school. More specifically, ActivityGram reports the amount of activity that a child performs, provides a graphical display of activity patterns, and indicates the types of activity performed by the child. This type of feedback helps students learn how to set up programs to increase their participation in moderate and vigorous physical activity, in strength and flexibility activities, and in lifestyle activities (i.e., activities of daily living). ActivityGram uses the Physical Activity Pyramid as a basis for analyzing personal activity patterns (see figure 1.1).

PROGRAM PHILOSOPHY: HELP

The mission, goals, and program components of FitnessGram are embedded in a unifying philosophy that guides both program development and software components: the HELP philosophy. This acronym reflects the philosophy that health (H) is available to everyone (E), is for a lifetime (L), and is personal (P). The HELP philosophy was developed by Chuck Corbin and has been presented as a core concept in his books, including *Fitness for Life* (Corbin and Le Masurier 2014; Corbin and Lindsey 2005). The individual components of the philosophy are described in the following paragraphs.

Health

Physical activity provides important health benefits and can enhance quality of life for both children and adults. More specifically, regular participation in physical activity produces improvement in multiple dimensions of health-related physical fitness: aerobic capacity; body composition; and muscular strength, endurance, and flexibility. The criterion-referenced standards used for these dimensions in FitnessGram are based on the level of fitness needed for good health. Similar activity guidelines used in ActivityGram are based on how active children should be for the purpose of optimal health.

Everyone

All children can be successful in FitnessGram. Whereas some physical fitness programs emphasize the attainment of high levels of performance on components of fitness, we believe that extremely high levels of physical fitness (though admirable) are not necessary for accomplishing objectives associated with good health and improved function. Rather, with reasonable amounts of physical activity, all children can receive sufficient health benefits. In a free society, individuals choose what they want to emphasize and where they want to strive for excellence. Some students decide to make such an effort in the sciences or in the arts; others (for example, athletes) give high priority to physical activity and fitness. We recognize this diversity as a good thing, and we view the FitnessGram program as a way to help all children and youth achieve a level of activity and fitness associated with good health, growth, and function.

Lifetime

Of course, in order to continue providing benefits, physical activity must be maintained over time. Lifetime physical activity, in turn, is determined largely by one's level of confidence in regard to skills and behaviors associated with physical activity—that is, one's self-efficacy. Therefore, assessments should be aimed at enhancing self-efficacy; more specifically, we discourage assessment activities that undermine self-efficacy but encourage assessments that improve perceptions of competence. To put it in more practical terms, we discourage inter-student comparisons of personal self-assessment data but encourage self-comparison of results over time and self-comparison with health standards.

Personal

Because fitness is personal, one must prioritize the privacy of results when using FitnessGram and ActivityGram. The data collected during the

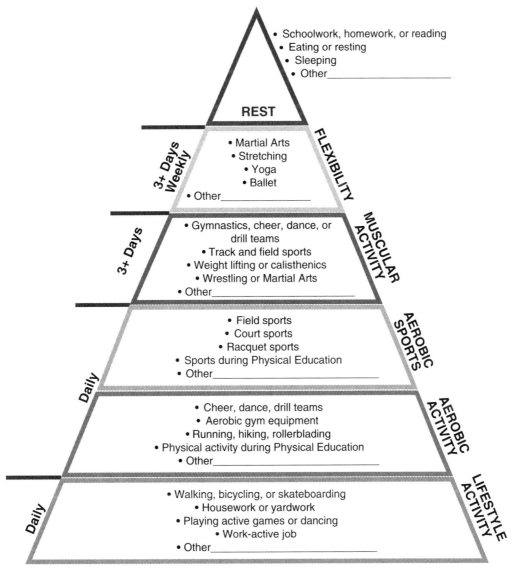

Figure 1.1 Physical Activity Pyramid used in ActivityGram.

assessments should be considered personal information, and appropriate care should be taken when administering the tests and discussing the results. Ensuring confidentiality helps individuals focus less on comparison with others and more on their own personal needs. Indeed, FitnessGram is designed for individual assessment and personalized feedback. Referencing the HELP philosophy throughout the fitness education process allows the teacher to incorporate goal-setting strategies and monitor progress with individual students.

 KEY CONCEPTS

- The mission of the FitnessGram program is to promote lifelong physical activity among youth.
- The specific goals of the FitnessGram program are to promote enjoyable, regular physical activity and to provide comprehensive physical fitness and physical activity assessments and reporting programs for children and youth.
- The FitnessGram program uses the HELP philosophy: "health is available to everyone for a lifetime—and it's personal."

2

Fitness Education and Assessment Guidelines

The long-term objective of a physical education program is to help students build the physical and behavioral skills they need in order to be active for life. In fact, this objective should be viewed as the culmination or final outcome of a well-executed K-12 curriculum. To reach this objective, most experts recommend using a hierarchical curriculum that builds with each passing year.

The recommended progression of physical skills in physical education can be likened to the progressions used to teach and reinforce reading. Just as students first learn basic words and sentences, they must also first master basic physical skills. As children develop, they need opportunities to start reading books; similarly, they need opportunities to practice and apply skills in games. With further development, students learn to read different types of material in order to learn about subjects of interest; in the same way, they can learn ways to enhance their skills and apply them to the sports and other activities that interest them most. Therefore, as in reading development, a child's physical development is best served by a systematic progression from year to year.

The recommended objectives at each level of development are highlighted by the conceptual diagram presented in figure 2.1. In the elementary years, emphasis should be placed on providing opportunities for children to experience and enjoy a variety of activities. It is critical at this stage for students to both learn and practice physical skills because doing so builds their self-efficacy and their perceptions of competence. Developing a good repertoire of skills also makes it easier for children to learn sports and other lifetime activities that they can perform as they get older. At the middle school level, the focus should shift to skill instruction so that children can master specific movement skills. Again, care should be taken to minimize experiences of failure, because long-term attitudes toward physical activity may begin to form at this age.

In high school, students should be given more choice about the activities they perform. In fact, the key to figure 2.1 lies in the fact that the scope of activities and the nature of instruction are both broadened throughout elementary school and into middle school and then taper off in high school. Therefore, though a given teacher may be involved with only a few grade levels, all teachers need to understand the recommended progression of experiences in physical education.

Behavioral skills must also be addressed in order to increase the chances that students will be active throughout their lives. Ultimately, students need to learn to self-assess their fitness, interpret assessment results, plan a personal program, and motivate themselves to remain active on their own. Instruction geared toward behavioral skills requires a K-12 progression similar to the one just described for physical skills. Tools for teaching these concepts are provided with the fitness and activity assessments in the FitnessGram program. Both the purpose of the assessments and the depth of coverage should be matched to children's interests and abilities. The following sections highlight the recommended uses and applications of the FitnessGram assessments in the physical education curriculum.

ASSESSMENT OPTIONS FOR FITNESS EDUCATION

The FitnessGram program helps evaluate—and educate youth about—levels of physical activity and physical fitness. The resulting information can be used in various ways, depending on the philosophy of the teacher, school, or district. Similarly, various assessment methods can be used, depending on the primary objective of a given physical education program. The following sections describe the more commonly used assessment options: individualized testing, self-testing, personal-best testing, and institutional testing.

Individualized Testing

Individualized testing provides students with accurate indicators of their fitness and physical activity. In physical education, students should learn whether or not they have sufficient fitness and are performing sufficient amounts of activity for good health. Appropriate health-related criteria provide the basis for the criterion-referenced standards used in both FitnessGram and ActivityGram. Specifically, the software and printed reports provide prescriptive feedback depending on whether the child attained the Healthy Fitness Zone (i.e., the objective, criterion-based standard) for a given dimension of fitness or amount of activity. Students who do *not* reach the Healthy Fitness Zone receive feedback to help them develop a program of improvement.

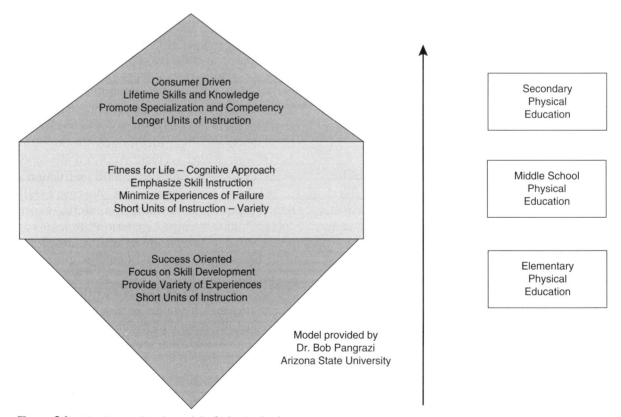

Figure 2.1 The hierarchical model of physical education.

Reprinted, by permission, from Dr. Bob Pangrazi, Department of Exercise Science & Physical Education, Arizona State University (Professor Emeritus), Education Specialist Gopher Sport.

Students who *do* reach the Healthy Fitness Zone receive information to help them maintain their fitness or activity level.

In some situations, the teacher may elect to have the student stop the test upon achieving a score equal to the upper limit of the Healthy Fitness Zone. Doing so can reduce the time required for testing and may also reduce the possibility of creating an embarrassing or threatening environment for students who are less capable or less fit. Parents should be informed about the process so that they understand that the performance reported on the child's FitnessGram does not necessarily represent a maximal effort.

One main goal of the FitnessGram program is to help keep parents informed about their child's level of health-related fitness and activity habits. The teacher can communicate individualized results to parents by sending the personalized report home to them and instructing them about how to interpret the results. This instruction can be provided in the form of a cover memo or direct interaction at parent–teacher conferences. Either way, the goal of this communication is to enhance parental involvement in promoting the child's physical activity (for more about promoting physical activity, see chapter 3). Parents should be encouraged to use the personalized messages to help students plan personal activity programs suited to individual needs. If parental feedback is provided, we recommend informing students so that they are aware that the results will be shared with their families. For older students especially, informing them indicates a respect for their privacy. Teachers should ensure that students understand their scores, how those scores relate to the Healthy Fitness Zone, and how to set physical activity goals that help them improve their performance. This process will be easier if the teacher uses the FitnessGram software and reports.

Results from the FitnessGram program can be charted over time to provide a personalized fitness portfolio. For example, a student's results can be plotted on a regular basis to show whether the student is retaining his or her fitness status; the goal is to help all youth meet or exceed criterion-referenced standards on all parts of fitness over time. In addition, when dramatic changes occur in personal performance, tracking helps the student, the teacher, and the parents identify reasons for the changes. Individual testing strategies are covered in the following subsections.

Self-Testing

Self-testing involves personal assessments made by individual students of their own fitness and activity levels. Students are taught to give the tests to themselves and to interpret their own test results. Once students become accomplished in self-testing, they can repeat the testing periodically to assess their improvement. Teaching self-testing is an important objective in physical education because it provides students with the necessary tools for testing themselves and planning personal programs throughout life. Effective self-testing requires a considerable amount of practice, which in turn necessitates multiple opportunities to practice.

Self-testing results are considered personal; therefore, a student's self-test information can be kept private if she or he so desires. With access to FitnessGram software, students can input personal test results in the privacy of their own home. Personal FitnessGram reports can still be printed, but students should decide for themselves whether they want to share their personal information. Test results for beginning self-testers are not particularly accurate, and this point should be emphasized to students and parents (if results are shared).

Personal-Best Testing

The FitnessGram philosophy focuses on good health, which does not require high levels of fitness. Some youth, however, are interested in achieving high levels of fitness in order to meet performance goals, and teachers may wish to give these students the opportunity for testing geared toward that objective. To that end, in personal-best testing, a student strives to achieve a personal-best score on a specific fitness test. This type of testing is not recommended for all students, because some children and youth are not interested in achieving especially high performance results. Therefore, personal-best testing is best performed either before or after school and on a voluntary basis.

Institutional Testing

Institutional testing refers to assessments conducted to help teachers determine the levels of activity, fitness, or both in a group of students. It is referred to as "institutional" testing because it may be required by a school or district as a way to document and track student outcomes. In order to be informative, tests used for this purpose must be administered consistently across classes and over time; therefore, this type of testing requires a more structured and formalized approach than is needed for either individualized testing or self-testing. Specifically, teachers must take care to adhere to the established FitnessGram test protocols in order to improve the reliability and validity of test results. In addition, because the assessments may require feedback and judgment in order to determine the number of repetitions completed, additional testers or assistants may be needed to help administer the tests and document results. This added structure takes additional time but is necessary if the results are to provide meaningful information.

If annual institutional testing is called for, it should always be done at the same time of year because fitness levels will fluctuate from the beginning to the end of the year. In addition, interpreting data obtained from this type of testing requires great care because many factors will influence student performance. More information on interpreting FitnessGram data may be found in chapter 10.

The results of fitness testing should not be used for determining student grades, long-term student achievement, or teacher success. As noted in the *FitnessGram/ActivityGram Reference Guide* (Plowman and Meredith 2013), fitness tests cannot be regarded as good indicators of student achievement because fitness is affected by many factors other than physical activity.

EFFECTIVE AND APPROPRIATE USE OF FITNESSGRAM AND ACTIVITYGRAM ASSESSMENTS IN PHYSICAL EDUCATION

This section outlines appropriate uses for FitnessGram and ActivityGram, identifies ways in which they should *not* be used, and presents recommendations for using the FitnessGram software in program evaluation.

Appropriate Uses of FitnessGram

The main purpose of FitnessGram is to provide each student, as well as the teacher and parents, with personal information about the student's current level of fitness. This information can be used as the basis for designing personal programs of fitness development. As described earlier, in order to meet students' changing developmental needs and address higher-order learning objectives, the

emphasis in physical education should progress as students move through the K-12 curriculum. The same is true for fitness testing. For example, at young ages, physical activity is not strongly linked to physical fitness; therefore, emphasis on structured fitness testing through FitnessGram is not recommended for children in grades K through 3. Instead, the goal in these grades should be to expose children to the various test items and help them learn about the various components of physical fitness. Self-testing, which is more informal, is recommended as the primary means to teach children about these assessments because they learn the specific elements of each test and are able to have unlimited practice.

In contrast, older elementary students can understand the different dimensions of fitness and may appreciate the feedback provided by the assessments. Therefore, though formal institutional testing is not necessarily recommended, structured individual testing can provide meaningful information for children, parents, and teachers. Later, in middle school and high school, the curriculum can include self-testing and both individual and periodic institutionalized testing. In order to avoid having students dread repetitive yearly testing, the emphasis should be changed across the years. For example, one year the focus could be on self-testing; individualized testing could be used the next year; and institutionalized testing could be done every third year.

Some teachers feel that conducting tests at the beginning of the year and again at the end of the year provides a good indication of student achievement. Although this type of testing may be used, the results must be interpreted with caution, for two reasons. First, as students get older, they improve regardless of whether they are doing physical activity; for this reason, incorrect messages may be conveyed (i.e., the year-end test might suggest improvement from physical education when in fact it resulted merely from growth). Second, if grades are based on performance improvement, students may learn to be intentionally "bad" on initial tests and then get "good" on later tests.

Appropriate Uses of ActivityGram

ActivityGram helps youth learn to monitor their own physical activity patterns in order to see how active they really are and to set goals for lifetime activity programs. These skills—self-monitoring, goal setting, and program planning—are referred to as self-management skills, and learning them is essential to sustaining physical activity for a lifetime (Dale and Corbin 2000; Dale, Corbin, and Cuddihy 1998).

The ActivityGram assessment requires the ability to recall bouts of physical activity or certain behavior over the past few days and to categorize activity by type, intensity, and duration. Therefore, it is not intended for use with children under the age of 10, who generally can recall their activities but have yet to develop robust concepts of time and perceptions of intensity. Students in older elementary grades may also have difficulty with the cognitive aspects of recall, so the emphasis with these children should be placed on the *process* of completing the assessments. Middle and high school students should be able to do the ActivityGram assessment without issue.

The ActivityGram module now includes ActivityGram Lite (Youth Activity Profile), a short survey developed at Iowa State University that allows students to report on the time spent being physically active at home and at school and time spent in sedentary behaviors. ActivityGram is a very thorough assessment of physical activity, but the three-day recall and data entry can be very time consuming. ActivityGram Lite offers an estimate of physical activity and sedentary behaviors using a short survey that requires much less time and data entry and can be quickly completed by groups of students.

ActivityGram can be used for institutional testing if standardized protocols are used for collecting the information, but proper consideration should be given to interpreting the accuracy of self-reported information. Teachers should understand that physical activity will be overestimated if students are not accurately recalling their activity.

Inappropriate Uses of FitnessGram and ActivityGram

The following list highlights inappropriate uses of FitnessGram and ActivityGram in physical education.

1. Student scores on FitnessGram and ActivityGram assessments should *not* be used to evaluate individual students in physical education, either for grading or for state-standards testing. Students differ in their interests and abilities, and grading them on fitness performance may involve holding them accountable for things beyond their control. In addition, posting results for other students to see can create an embarrassing situation that does little to foster positive attitudes toward activity.

2. Student scores on FitnessGram and ActivityGram assessments should *not* be used to evaluate teacher effectiveness—that is, for conducting teacher evaluations. Teachers can be effective at teaching youngsters how to develop and maintain physical fitness and still have students who do not perform well on fitness tests. Furthermore, physical education teachers who emphasize *only* fitness activities may shortchange their students in other areas, such as developing motor skills, social skills, and positive attitudes toward physical activity.

Of course, tools such as the FitnessGram program can support a high-quality physical education program and help increase teacher effectiveness. However, when evaluating teacher effectiveness, it is appropriate to turn to the Society of Health and Physical Educators (SHAPE America, formerly known as the American Alliance for Health, Physical Education, Recreation, and Dance, or AAHPERD) and the National Association for Sport and Physical Education (NASPE). These two groups have created the Physical Education Teacher Evaluation Tool (NASPE 2007), which can guide administrators in developing evaluation criteria for physical education teachers. The tool addresses the following categories: quality of instruction (e.g., use of differentiation and technology to aid learning), evidence of student learning (e.g., formative and summative assessment, communication of results to individual students), positive learning climate (e.g., confidentiality of fitness scores, high expectations for learning and behavior), classroom management, and professionalism.

3. Student scores on FitnessGram and ActivityGram assessments should *not* be used to evaluate the overall quality of physical education—that is, for program assessment. Promoting physical fitness is only one part of a high-quality physical education program. As stated at the outset of this chapter, the ultimate goal of physical education is to promote lifelong physical activity, which also requires the teaching of physical skills, cooperative skills, and health-maintenance skills.

The National Association for Sport and Physical Education (NASPE), which is now part of SHAPE America, offers several tools that provide appropriate measures for physical education programs. For example, Physical Education Program Checklist (SHAPE America 2015) includes a physical education program assessment. Many of the questions can be addressed through the FitnessGram program.

 HOW TO APPLY

Recommended Approaches for Program Evaluation

For better or worse, there is an increasing emphasis in the United States on standardized testing in schools, and physical education is no exception. Education programs at all levels are increasingly being asked to document how they monitor progress and achieve stated learning objectives. This focus has created a need to develop a systematic approach to documenting important outcomes in physical education. Teachers should refer to the *National Standards and Grade-Level Outcomes for K-12 Physical Education* (SHAPE America 2014) when determining how to evaluate the physical education program.

Some districts are interested in tracking trends over time. For example, changes in passing rates can provide useful information for curriculum planning. Program coordinators can also compare fitness and activity levels of similarly aged children in order to evaluate the utility of new lessons or initiatives. This type of documentation can help provide accountability for an overall program. To support such efforts, the FitnessGram software provides a number of tracking and reporting functions that facilitate documentation of group results. Additional information about program evaluation guidelines can be found in the *FitnessGram/ActivityGram Reference Guide* (Plowman and Meredith 2013). Schools and districts are encouraged to carefully consider the relative merits of different evaluation criteria. Emphasis should be placed on quality-improvement approaches that seek to systematically improve overall programs.

THE FITNESS EDUCATION PROCESS: STEP BY STEP

The fitness education process consists of eight steps (see figure 2.2), beginning with instruction about activity and fitness concepts and ending with revision and readjustment of the physical activity program. Let's look at the steps in some detail.

1. **Instruction about activity and fitness concepts.** Students should be instructed in basic concepts of fitness development and maintenance, including the following:

- Importance of regular exercise to health and to prevention of degenerative disease
- Description of each area of fitness and its importance to health
- Methods for developing each area of fitness

2. **Student participation in conditioning activities.** If fitness testing is conducted, students should be preconditioned for testing in order to maximize safety. *Hint:* This work can be facilitated by the Get Fit Conditioning Program—materials are available in the accompanying web resource (see figure 2.3, *a* and *b*). You can do some of the activities in class and assign others for completion during students' leisure time.

3. **Instruction about test items.** When teaching each test item, include the following elements:

- Why it is important for health
- What it measures
- How to administer it
- Practice sessions

Hint: View the FitnessGram test protocol videos in the web resource with your class.

4. **Assessment of fitness levels.** If possible, allow students to test one another or have a team of parents assist in conducting the assessments. Also, teach students to conduct self-assessments.

5. **Planning the fitness program and setting goals.** After completing the fitness testing, use the results to help each student set goals and plan his or her personal fitness program. Activity goals can emphasize areas in which the student has the greatest need. Include the following elements:

Additional Resources

A copy of the FitnessGram position on appropriate and inappropriate uses of fitness and activity assessment can be found in the *FitnessGram/ActivityGram Reference Guide* (Plowman and Meredith 2013), which can be downloaded at www.cooperinstitute.org/reference-guide. This position statement is also available in the web resource for this manual.

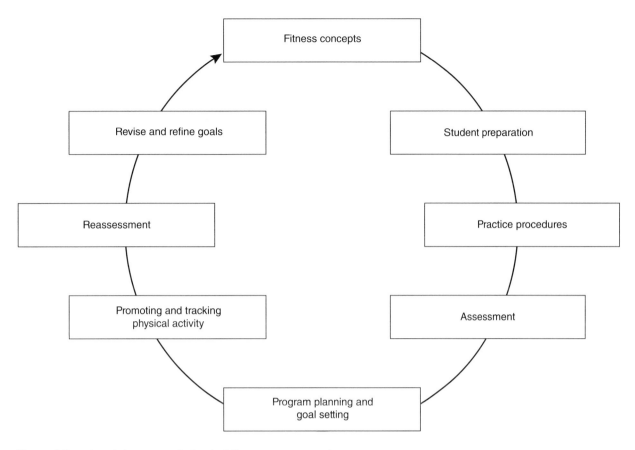

Figure 2.2 The eight steps of physical fitness programming.

This process evolved from the planning process originated by Corbin and cited in Corbin et al. 2016.

- Teach students how to interpret their results.
- Help students set process goals for an exercise program to improve or maintain their fitness or activity levels (for more on goal setting with students, see chapter 11).
- Evaluate group performance on each test item.

Hint for software users: Use the FitnessGram reports to inform students and parents of results.

6. **Promoting and tracking physical activity.** Make every effort to motivate students to establish regular physical activity habits; also recognize students for success in their efforts.

Allow time during physical education for students to work toward their goals but also expect them to spend some of their leisure time participating in fun activities that help them achieve their goals. The

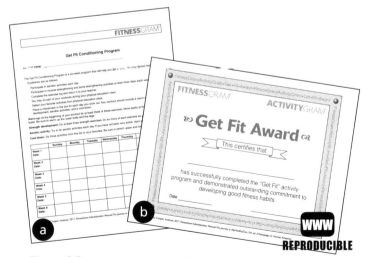

Figure 2.3 The Get Fit Conditioning Program materials, which are available in the accompanying web resource, include (a) instructions and (b) award.

key is for students to have fun while participating in physical activity.

Hint for software users: ActivityLog can help students learn how to monitor their physical activity level. At the same time, periodic use of the Activity-Gram assessment can provide more comprehensive evaluation of overall activity patterns.

7. **Reassessment.** Periodic reassessment informs students about how they are changing and reinforces for them the practice of "sticking with it." Recognition for achieving goals is a vital part of establishing behavior patterns.

Hint: When you report results, show individual progress by using individualized reports; show group progress by using a group statistical report. Both kinds of reports can be used to show changes in scores from the previous test period, thus helping to evaluate progress.

8. **Revision.** Once reassessment yields new information, you can revise or refine goals. Provide individualized feedback to students so that they know what areas to focus on. At the same time, work toward the major instructional goal of teaching students how to evaluate their own results and set their own personal goals.

PHYSICAL EDUCATION RESOURCES TO SUPPORT USE OF FITNESSGRAM

Among the various physical education curricula available, some have direct conceptual and philosophical links with the FitnessGram program. This section describes three examples: Physical Best, Fitness for Life, and the Presidential Youth Fitness Program.

Physical Best

Physical Best is a companion product to the FitnessGram program. Developed by SHAPE America, Physical Best is a complete educational program for teaching health-related fitness concepts. It includes learning activities in the following areas of health-related fitness: aerobic fitness, body composition, muscular strength and endurance, and flexibility. The curriculum also includes components that can be used to promote parent and community involvement. Physical Best is a unique physical education curriculum in a number of ways.

Using the Fitness Education Process to Teach Physical Education and Increase Personal Fitness

Spotlight on FitnessGram and ActivityGram

Ginny Popiolek
Supervisor of Health and Elementary/Middle Physical Education
Harford County Public Schools, Baltimore, Maryland

The Harford County Public Schools have used Fitness-Gram at the district level since 2004. The use of FitnessGram has created a paradigm shift that promotes physical activity over a lifetime by helping educators create personalized goal-setting and student-wellness plans that are enhanced by education and assessment. More specifically, the wellness plans help raise awareness of physical activity guidelines, recommendations, and students' current fitness levels.

We begin the assessment process by educating students about the importance of activity and fitness. Focusing on the why and how helps students develop a sense of personal responsibility and commitment. Next, we administer a pre-test to give students a baseline measurement. We then conduct a goal-setting lesson, and students set personal goals and create a wellness plan using their baseline data.

On a larger scale, departments use FitnessGram to analyze schoolwide data, looking for strengths and weaknesses and aligning instruction appropriately. For example, if upper-body strength is found to be low among seventh graders, we can adjust warm-ups to allow more time to address the strength concern. We also use fitness data in creating curricular learning objectives as part of the Race to the Top program (a competitive grant program for innovation funded by the United States Department of Education).

Fitness is reassessed at the end of the year, whereupon reports can be e-mailed to parents and guardians. In addition, physicians have been alerted to the availability of this information through the local health department and certain professional development groups. As a result, physicians are asking parents for the report in order to reflect the results in students' annual check-ups.

- It is inclusive in that it provides developmentally appropriate activities for different ages and abilities.

- It is personal in the way that it focuses on each child's individual preferences and capabilities.

- It is criterion-referenced in its use of established health guidelines to emphasize personal improvement rather than unrealistic performance-based standards.

- It teaches cognitive knowledge through physical activity.

- It was created by teachers for teachers; it resulted from the work of practitioners who have used the activities and teaching methods in the classroom.

- Its ongoing development is guided by a steering committee of SHAPE America members.

These characteristics—combined with FitnessGram—form a comprehensive program that provides one-stop shopping for physical activity, nutrition education, and assessment in fitness education. Physical Best is also linked to SHAPE America's national physical education standards and learning outcomes, thus providing educators with accountability. It includes resources appropriate to every K-12 grade level.

Fitness for Life

Fitness for Life is a comprehensive K-12 program that helps students take responsibility for their own activity, fitness, and health and prepares them to be physically active and healthy throughout their adult lives. This standards-based program is carefully articulated and follows a pedagogically sound scope and sequence to enhance student learning and progress. The program includes three sets of coordinated resources:

- A K-6 program addressing nutrition, physical activity, and wellness

- A personal-fitness text for middle school students

- The nation's first personal-fitness textbook for teens, now in its sixth edition (Corbin and Le Masurier 2014)

Fitness for Life is designed to be integrated with other physical education activities in order to create a high-quality, comprehensive physical education program. Fitness for Life is also fully integrated with both Physical Best and FitnessGram, and it shares the same HELP philosophy (see chapter 1 of this manual). The Fitness for Life materials contain specific guidelines that help students learn how to evaluate and interpret their own fitness scores (based on FitnessGram assessments) and how to build the behavioral skills needed for lifetime fitness. Thus the program provides an ideal way to achieve higher-level learning outcomes in both elementary and secondary physical education.

Presidential Youth Fitness Program

The Presidential Youth Fitness Program (PYFP) was developed to ensure that what happens before, during, and after a fitness assessment is beneficial to students and teachers and helps youth be active for life. The program provides a model for fitness education within a comprehensive, high-quality physical education program. It includes the following resources and tools to help physical educators enhance their fitness education process:

- FitnessGram health-related fitness assessment

- Instructional strategies to promote student physical activity and fitness

- Communication tools to help physical educators increase awareness about their work in the classroom

- Options for recognizing individuals' achievements in fitness and physical activity

In these ways, PYFP supports physical educators in following the SHAPE America national standards and grade-level outcomes for physical education in order to develop physically literate individuals.

KEY CONCEPTS

- Physical activity and health-related fitness can be evaluated at the individual level through self-testing, peer testing, and personal-best testing. Institutional testing, on the other hand, allows teachers to view group data for the purposes of curriculum development and program planning.

- The following guidelines help ensure appropriate use of fitness testing data: teach the components of health-related fitness as part of a high-quality physical education program, provide feedback to students and parents, and use assessment data to guide program planning in physical education.

- The fitness education process provides educators with a way to collect data and inform others about physical fitness. It also helps individuals learn to plan lifelong physical activity programs to maintain and improve their overall fitness.

- Resources are available to help you advocate for effective and appropriate use of fitness data.

3

Promoting Physical Activity

The benefits of an active lifestyle have been recognized for a long time, but the importance of physical activity in particular has received greater attention in recent years. Much of this attention has been prompted by the highly publicized epidemic of obesity affecting the United States and most other developed countries. Childhood obesity has more than doubled in children and quadrupled in adolescents over the past 30 years; furthermore, these trends are consistent across all age groups, both sexes, and all races and ethnicities. The increasing prevalence of overweight in children has raised considerable concern, in part because it is well established that overweight and obesity tend to track throughout the life span.

This chapter describes the rationale for promoting physical activity in physical education. It also presents the youth physical activity promotion model to illustrate different ways in which teachers can promote children's physical activity behavior. The last section of the chapter addresses the value of recognition systems in rewarding and promoting physical activity behavior.

IMPORTANCE OF PROMOTING PHYSICAL ACTIVITY IN PHYSICAL EDUCATION

Over the years, the goals and objectives of physical education have evolved to fit prevailing views about the contributions of physical activity and fitness to health and well-being. In recent years, a shift in public health policy toward the importance of regular physical activity has led to changes in physical education. Whereas physical fitness is still considered an important goal for physical education, the general consensus now holds that it is more important to focus on promoting the process (behavior) of physical activity than on the product (outcome), which is fitness. One primary reason for this shift lies in the fact that physical activity has the potential to track into adulthood. Fitness, on the other hand, is transient and is maintained only if an individual remains physically active. Therefore, the key role of physical education is to promote lifetime physical activity.

Communicating the importance of physical activity to children may be difficult if fitness testing is used as the sole form of evaluation in the physical education curriculum. For example, if a child scores well on fitness testing without being active, he or she may believe that it is not necessary to be active on a regular basis. Conversely, children who are active but score poorly on fitness tests may lose confidence and develop negative attitudes toward physical activity. Therefore, in order to promote lifetime physical activity, we must provide direct instruction about—and reinforcement of—not the intended outcome but the behavior itself. This conceptual shift in physical education can be facilitated by incorporating messages about the need for regular physical activity into FitnessGram, ActivityGram, and ActivityLog. Though children can learn about the relationship between physical activity and physical fitness through the FitnessGram program, it is also incumbent upon the physical education teacher to help promote lifetime physical activity in children.

PHYSICAL ACTIVITY GUIDELINES

The Physical Activity Guidelines for Americans, issued by the U.S. Department of Health and Human Services (HHS 2008), include behavioral targets to help children adopt a healthy, active lifestyle.

The guidelines for children differ from those for adults because children themselves are different from adults. The amount of activity recommended for children (60 minutes daily) is greater than the amount recommended for adults (150 minutes of moderate-intensity activity or 75 minutes of vigorous-intensity activity every week) because children have more available time in the day and because they need to establish active patterns and develop motor skills early in life. The guidelines are also geared toward reducing inactivity among children because excessive inactivity (e.g., screen time) contributes to obesity and reduces opportunities for physical activity.

The following list summarizes the current youth portion of the guidelines (HHS 2008). However, we strongly recommended that you read the original document and seek to apply the guidelines in your teaching. Children and adolescents should engage in one hour or more of physical activity per day, and their activity should be spread across the following types.

- Aerobic: A majority of physical activity time for children and adolescents should be spent in activity of moderate or vigorous intensity. In addition, on at least three days per week, the activity should be vigorous (e.g., running, hopping, skipping, jumping rope, swimming, dancing, bicycling).
- Muscle-strengthening: On at least three days per week, children and adolescents should perform muscle-strengthening physical activity—that is, activity that makes their muscles do more work than is usual during daily life. This activity may be either structured (e.g., doing push-ups, curl-ups, and other calisthenics in physical education; lifting weights) or unstructured (e.g., using playground equipment, climbing trees, playing tug of war).
- Bone-strengthening: On at least three days per week, children and adolescents should perform bone-strengthening physical activity—that is, activity that puts force on the bones, thereby promoting bone growth (e.g., running, jumping rope, playing basketball, playing hopscotch).

In pursuing this goal, children and adolescents should be encouraged to participate in activities that are enjoyable, age appropriate, and variable in type.

Given that the central goal of physical education is to promote lifetime physical activity, we must abide by and work to achieve established public-health guidelines for physical activity. The Physical Activity Guidelines for Americans (HHS 2008) call for children to participate in 60 minutes of physical activity each day of the week. The guidelines acknowledge that moderate-intensity physical activity can provide significant health benefits even if performed intermittently throughout the day. Emphasis is placed on helping all individuals be somewhat active rather than on promoting high levels of activity in subsamples of the population.

It is well established that children are the most active segment of the population, but individual activity levels are known to decrease during adolescence. Studies have also shown dramatic increases in sedentary behavior as children move from elementary school to middle school and then on to high school; some of these changes come about as adolescents begin to take on adult responsibilities and adult lifestyle patterns. One challenge, then, is to maintain a child's natural interest in activity over time (HHS 2014). Strategies for doing so can be found in the youth physical activity promotion model described in a later section of this chapter.

CONCEPTS FOR PROMOTING SCHOOL PHYSICAL ACTIVITY

There is a clear consensus among public health experts that lifestyle behaviors are influenced by many factors, some of which lie beyond an individual's control. For example, education and behavior-change programming are unlikely to produce long-term effects without broader social and environmental supports. With this in mind, comprehensive social ecological models of health promotion (see figure 3.1) are widely endorsed in public-health work because they capture the interconnected influences on behavior. The various models of this type share the understanding that behaviors can be influenced at multiple levels: individual, interpersonal, organizational, community, and policy. In other words, the models depict the nested nature of society; that is, individuals are nested within groups (e.g., families, classes), which are nested within organizations (e.g., churches, schools, worksites), which in turn are nested within communities. The main concept of social ecological models, then, is that targeting multiple levels makes it possible to influence behavior more comprehensively.

Historically, physical education has been geared to the individual or interpersonal level as instruction and feedback have typically been provided to individual students in small-group settings. In the broader social-ecological approach, however, teachers can exert greater influence by adopting an expanded role, both as facilitators of family- and community-based physical activity and as champions of public policies that support high-quality physical education and physical activity programs for children.

As shown in figure 3.1, physical education teachers are ideally positioned to exert influence on all levels of the social ecological framework. For example, they can directly affect and contribute to

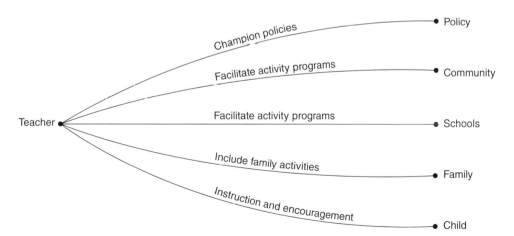

Figure 3.1 This social ecological model (SEM) shows a vision of the role that physical educators can play as school- and community-level promoters of physical activity in order to engage all levels of influence on a student.

Adapted from CDC. Available: www.cdc.gov/obesity/health_equity/addressingtheissue.html

school policies related to physical education (i.e., the policy level). They can also exert influence at the community level by working to create school and community environments conducive to physical activity. Programming through the physical activity curriculum (e.g., providing activity challenges) is viewed as organizational-level activity because it is coordinated separately for individual groups (i.e., school classes). Perhaps most important, teachers can affect people at the interpersonal level by working to promote family involvement in physical education at school. Though it is important to provide opportunities for youth to be active during school (which is a way of working at the individual level), youth are unlikely to accumulate the recommended amount of activity (60 minutes per day) solely through school. Therefore, they also need to be active outside of school, which is more likely to happen when teachers promote family involvement.

This type of expanded vision led to the development of the comprehensive school physical activity program (CSPAP) in 2013. CSPAP is an approach to physical education developed by the U.S. Centers for Disease Control and Prevention (CDC) in collaboration with the Society of Health and Physical Educators of America (SHAPE America). *Comprehensive School Physical Activity Program: A Guide for Schools* was published in 2013 (HHS 2013) to provide schools and school districts a step-by-step guide for developing, implementing, and evaluating comprehensive school physical activity programs. The CSPAP approach encourages, and reinforces the importance of, being physically active for a lifetime. The approach includes five major components:

- Physical education
  - Use of standards-based instruction
  - Moderate to vigorous physical activity for at least 50 percent of class time
  - Developmentally appropriate activity
  - Qualified teachers
  - Community and parental support
- Physical activity during school
  - Morning activity break
  - Daily walk time
  - Integration of movement into academic content
  - Recess
  - Encouragement of organized physical activity after lunch

One District's Comprehensive School Physical Activity Program
Spotlight on FitnessGram and ActivityGram

Karin Klemm
Health and Physical Education Coordinator
McKinney Independent School District (ISD), McKinney, Texas

McKinney ISD has found success in promoting physical activity and health through the use of morning activity breaks (during school announcements), in-class activity breaks, recess, and after-school sport and activity clubs. Meanwhile, our physical education program has been enhanced by FitnessGram, which allows us to use assessments and health-related standards to drive instruction and advocate for high-quality physical education.

In addition, our staff members are actively involved in our school health advisory council and participate in staff wellness activities. We also participate in many activities that promote physical activity for staff and community members, including Walk to School Day, fitness nights, schoolwide health fairs, our community 5K, and the city's health fair. These partnerships with the city, as well as local hospitals and fitness facilities, engage the community in our efforts to promote a healthy and active lifestyle.

- Physical activity before and after school
  - Intramural sport
  - Interscholastic sport
  - Physical activity clubs (e.g., running, biking)
  - Youth sport
  - Active travel to and from school
- Staff involvement
  - Staff wellness program
  - Role modeling for students
  - Sponsorship of physical activities (e.g., intramurals, physical activity clubs)
- Family and community engagement
  - Community access to school facilities (e.g., gym, playground)
  - Promotion of programs to parents (e.g., walking clubs)
  - Partnership with community-based programs
  - Dissemination of information (e.g., newsletter, Facebook posts, blogs)

The vision of expanding school-activity promotion efforts has also been highlighted in a prominent report titled *Educating the Student Body: Taking Physical Activity and Physical Education to School* (Institute of Medicine 2013). Teachers are encouraged to obtain access to the CSPAP and IOM documents to learn more about how to most effectively promote physical activity across the school day.

THE YOUTH PHYSICAL ACTIVITY PROMOTION MODEL

The youth physical activity promotion model (figure 3.2; Welk 1999) summarizes the various factors that influence children's interest and involvement in physical activity. Specifically, the model helps us promote physical activity in children by distinguishing between factors that predispose, factors that enable, and factors that reinforce activity behavior in children.

Predisposing Factors

Predisposing factors influence physical activity behavior in terms of two fundamental questions: "Is it worth it?" and "Am I able?" The question "Is it worth it?" addresses the benefits versus the costs of participating in physical activity. This question reflects children's attitudes toward physical activity and the level of enjoyment they get from movement experiences. The question "Am I able?" addresses perceptions of competence; in other words, it is possible for a child to value physical activity yet feel incapable of competently performing a given activity. Because it is part of human nature to want to display competence and hide incompetence, children who feel unskilled at physical activity may not want to be active. Therefore, children must be able to answer yes to both questions in order to be predisposed to physical activity.

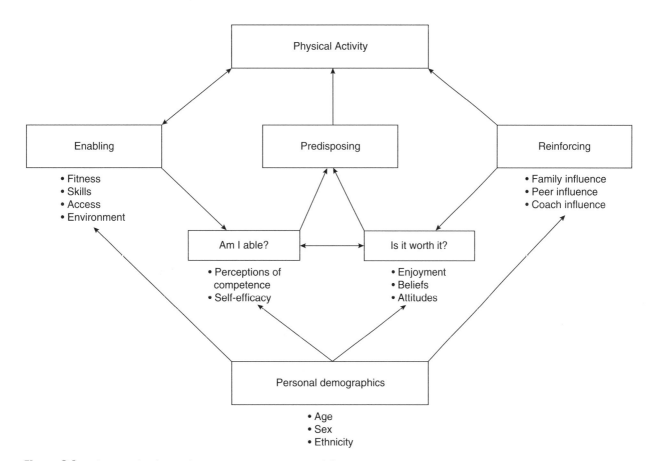

Figure 3.2 The youth physical activity promotion model.

Adapted, by permission, from G. Welk, 1999, "The youth physical activity promotion model: A conceptual bridge between theory and practice," *Quest* 51: 5-23.

Enabling Factors

Enabling factors include environmental variables, physical skills, physical fitness, and self-perceptions of competence. Environmental variables include access to facilities, equipment, and programs that provide opportunities for physical activity. Although these variables can directly influence a child's level of physical activity, they do not ensure participation; that is, children who have access may or may not choose to use the opportunity. However, children who do *not* have access lack even the opportunity to choose whether to use such resources. Other enabling factors include physical skills and physical fitness. Children who are physically skilled and fit are more likely to seek out opportunities to be active, whereas children with poor skills and poor fitness are less likely to do so. This tendency is most likely effected through children's perceptions of competence (i.e., the "Am I able?" question addressed in the discussion of predisposing factors). A child's perception of competence can greatly affect her or his level of attraction to physical activity; in fact, research has shown that perceptions of competence may be even more important than competence itself. Fortunately, teachers can directly promote skills through effective instruction and constructive feedback.

Reinforcing Factors

Reinforcing factors are variables that reinforce both a child's interest and his or her involvement in physical activity. The child's activity behavior can be affected by reinforcement from parents, peers, teachers, and coaches. Reinforcing factors can influence a child's physical activity behavior either directly or indirectly. A direct effect, for example, might be exerted by a parent or teacher who encourages a child to be physically active. An indirect effect, in contrast, might result from forces that shape a child's predisposition to physical activity, either in terms of interest ("Is it worth it?") or in terms of the child's perceived competence ("Am I able?"). At young ages, children may be more responsive to influence from teachers and parents; at older ages, peers probably exert a greater influence.

APPLYING THE YOUTH PHYSICAL ACTIVITY PROMOTION MODEL

The paths proposed in figure 3.2 suggest that physical activity can be promoted in a variety of ways. The central influence on activity behavior lies in the predisposing factors because this domain reflects the child's personal attitudes toward and perceptions of physical activity. Therefore, in order to most effectively promote interest and involvement in physical activity, physical education should emphasize experiences that promote children's enjoyment of physical activity ("It is worth it!") and perceptions of competence ("I am able!"). Toward this end, the Council on Physical Education for Children (1998) provided a set of guidelines for ensuring that physical activities are developmentally appropriate for children. We encourage educators to seek out this resource to help create programs that are educationally and motivationally sound for children.

Individual or Intrapersonal Promotion of Activity

As described in chapter 1, the FitnessGram program is rooted in the HELP philosophy: health (H) is for everyone (E), is for a lifetime (L), and is personal (P). In this philosophy, the primary objective of a fitness development program should be to help participants establish regular activity habits through enjoyable physical activity experiences. The overall, long-term fitness objective for all students should be to develop and maintain a level of fitness within the Healthy Fitness Zone. However, since being healthy is not a meaningful objective for most young children, the emphasis when working with them should be placed on objectives that are more relevant to their daily lives—for example, looking and feeling good. By the time children are in high school, an effort should be made to help them understand that physical activity is necessary for good health. One key concept to communicate at that point is that maintaining a healthy fitness level does not require a tremendous amount of activity or time. Therefore, even individuals who are not athletes and are not attracted to physical activity can easily do an adequate amount of activity to be healthy.

HOW TO APPLY

One unique aspect of the FitnessGram software is that it allows students (through the student version of the program) to view their own fitness results. The software helps students learn more about the various dimensions of fitness and the importance of regular physical activity. In addition, students learn that fitness is personal; in fact, because of this educational value for students, we advocate that students log in to the system and view their results.

Here are some additional recommendations for promoting physical activity and physical fitness on the individual level through physical education:

- Provide a rationale for children to participate in regular physical activity. Make the reasons relevant to their daily life; specifically, the benefits of looking good, feeling good, and enjoying life are usually most salient with children.

- Provide feedback regarding current status. Use test results to educate students about physical activity and fitness and to identify areas in which they can improve performance or maintain good performance.

- Encourage students to establish both short-term and long-term goals. Short-term goals are probably most important and should relate to physical activity rather than to achievement of fitness. The reason? If a student works hard toward improving fitness but does not manage to achieve a **product-oriented goal**, the result is a feeling of failure. In contrast, a process-oriented goal allows the student to succeed while slowly progressing toward the desired result (i.e., product). For example, instead of setting a product goal of doing five more sit-ups on the next test, set a **process goal** of performing abdominal strengthening activities three or four times per week. Goal-setting activities are available in the web resource.

- Help each student identify a regular time and place to fit physical activity into his or her daily schedule. Talk about fitting activities into daily routines—for example, by walking or biking to school, to a friend's house, or to the store. A major way to make time for physical activity is to reduce the amount of screen time (including TV, computer, and phones).

- Have each student make a written commitment to participate in the activity that is required in order to achieve her or his goal. The activity should be enjoyable to the student, and the written commitment should indicate the type of activity, day(s) of the week, time(s) of day, place(s), and other specific details.

- Encourage students to track their participation by means of a personal exercise log or the ActivityLog component of the FitnessGram software. Periodically assess students' physical activity levels using ActivityGram or ActivityGram Lite (Youth Activity Profile). Teachers without access to the software can use the monthly activity log (figure 3.3) and challenge activities (figure 3.4, a–c) in the web resource to develop physical-activity tracking projects for students.

- Show that you are seriously interested in the program by periodically asking students about their progress.

- Discuss progress and problems. Being active is not easy for some individuals. If a student has difficulty meeting a goal, ask other students to suggest solutions.

- Praise students even for small accomplishments in their efforts to achieve their goals. Feedback about success is very important in helping children feel competent and thus in establishing intrinsic motivation.

- Recommend activities of low to moderate intensity (e.g., walking, recreational bike riding) since they are more likely to be maintained than are some team-sport activities.

- Serve as a role model for your class by including regular activity as a part of your own lifestyle. Tell your students about your enjoyment of physical activity and its benefits.

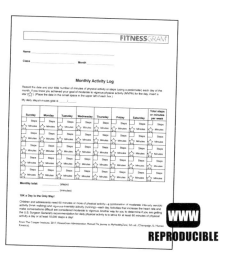

Figure 3.3 The monthly activity log is included in the accompanying web resource.

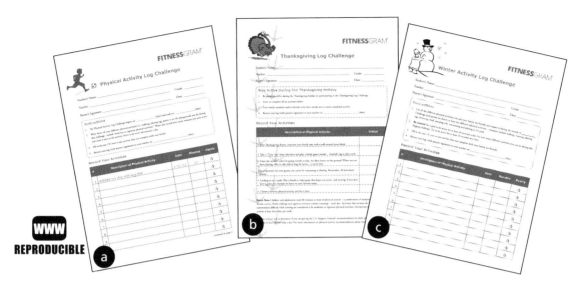

WWW
REPRODUCIBLE

Figure 3.4 Challenge activities to develop physical-activity tracking projects for students: *(a)* physical activity log, *(b)* Thanksgiving activity log, and *(c)* winter activity log.

Interpersonal and Institutional Promotion of Physical Activity

Promotion of physical activity must extend beyond the school and the school day and into the home and community. Toward this end, collaborative efforts between schools and community programs have been highlighted by the U.S. Centers for Disease Control and Prevention (2013) in a document titled *Comprehensive School Physical Activity Programs: A Guide for Schools.* These guidelines recommend promoting physical activity through a coordinated school health program that establishes links between school, family, and community. The process of developing these links should include a central role for physical educators. Thus, in this approach, the role of physical education broadens to include outreach goals that integrate school, family, and community programs.

HOW TO APPLY Here are some ways in which teachers can promote physical activity outside of school.

- Teach parents about their important role in shaping their child's interest in and enjoyment of physical activity. Ideally, families engage in physical activity together—for example, in the form of enjoyable evening and weekend outings. If the whole family cannot participate together, encourage activity performed in pairs.
- Encourage family support of children's efforts to be active. For example, parents can transport children to activity sessions and take them to

parks to play. Children can also be asked to help parents with chores so that parents have time for physical activity. Praise and encouragement are more effective than nagging.

- Involve parents as much as possible in promotional efforts through the vehicle of physical education. Ways of encouraging parental involvement include sending home FitnessGram and ActivityGram reports and providing parents with e-mail updates and reminders about promoting physical activity.
- Get connected to recreation and sport programs available in the community. Provide in-service training for volunteer coaches so that they become more aware of how to promote not just sport success but also lifelong activity in children.

To learn more, use the resources provided by national physical activity programs (see the sidebar titled "Samples of National Physical Activity Programs").

REINFORCEMENT: RECOGNITION AND MOTIVATION

One integral purpose of fitness and activity programs is to motivate children and youth to engage in sufficient activity to produce desired fitness outcomes. One method for motivating participants is to recognize them for their successes, and the FitnessGram

Samples of National Physical Activity Programs

- Let's Move! Active Schools—This comprehensive program empowers parents and schools to create active environments for students. The program provides schools with tools and resources, grants, direct assistance, and training to help students get moving and reach their greatest potential. To learn more, visit the program website at http://letsmoveschools.org.

- Comprehensive school physical activity program—SHAPE America recommends that all schools implement a CSPAP. Teachers may find key recommendations for implementing such a program for children and adolescents in *Comprehensive School Physical Activity Program: A Guide for Schools* (HHS 2013). To learn more, visit www.cdc.gov/healthyyouth/physicalactivity/cspap.htm.

- Alliance for a Healthier Generation—This organization's Healthy Schools Program brings parents, school staff, and students together to turn campuses into healthier places. To learn more, visit www.healthiergeneration.org.

- Presidential Youth Fitness Program (PYFP)—This program provides resources and tools to help physical educators enhance fitness education. To learn more, visit www.pyfp.org.

- PLAY 60 Challenge—This program offered by the American Heart Association and the National Football League inspires kids to get the recommended 60 total minutes of physical activity per day in school and at home. To learn more, visit www.heart.org.

- Fuel Up to Play 60 (FUTP60)—Founded by the National Dairy Council in collaboration with the U.S. Department of Agriculture, this program includes activities and funding to empower students to take charge of their health and fitness by making small, everyday changes at school. To learn more, visit www.fueluptoplay60.com.

program encourages a focus on *process*-based recognition in physical education. This approach relies on the fact that—to the extent allowed by heredity, maturation, and other factors—children and youth who are consistently active (i.e., who stick with the process) generally achieve good fitness (i.e., the product). *Performance*-based recognition is also acceptable but generally should not be used to the exclusion of recognition for being regularly active. The following paragraphs present the rationale for using a system of recognition based on behavior rather than on performance.

- To be effective, recognition must be based on achievement of goals that are challenging yet attainable. Goals that are too hard to reach are not motivating and can result in lack of effort. This is especially true for students with low physical self-esteem, who are often the very ones most in need of improved fitness. In contrast, challenging yet achievable goals are intrinsically motivating.

- If unattainable goals prevent an individual's efforts from seeming to pay off, he or she may develop "learned helplessness" and perceive no reason to keep trying. The best way to treat learned helplessness is to reward mastery *attempts* (i.e., effort or process) rather than mastery per se (i.e., performance or product).

- For any behavior, including exercise and physical fitness behaviors, intrinsic motivation must be based on continuous feedback—that is, information—about progress. Daily recognition of behavior can provide intrinsically motivating feedback about progress, personal achievement, and competence. Intrinsic motivation is evidenced by feelings of competence, willingness to give effort, a perception that exercise is important, lack of anxiety regarding activity, and enjoyment of activity.

Even so, awards and other forms of recognition are common in many youth fitness and sport programs. We must consider carefully, however, their developmental appropriateness and their consequences—both intended and unintended—in light of the goal of helping youth undertake lifelong engagement in physical activity. Let's now examine two recognition programs that align with the FitnessGram philosophy: the Presidential Youth Fitness Program and the Presidential Active Lifestyle Award.

Presidential Youth Fitness Program

The Presidential Youth Fitness Program (PYFP) supports high-quality physical education, promotes education about and awareness of physical fitness, and motivates and empowers youth to adopt and maintain healthy habits of regular physical activity. Central components of the PYFP program include the FitnessGram and ActivityGram assessments, which provide participants and organizers with information about youth physical activity and fitness levels. PYFP gives schools multiple options if they wish to recognize students who meet FitnessGram's criterion-based standards for physical fitness. Examples include printing students' names in school newsletters and providing students with certificates or digital badges. The two primary PYFP award options are as follows:

- The Presidential Youth Fitness Award recognizes students who achieve the Healthy Fitness Zone standard in at least five of six FitnessGram test categories.

- The Presidential Active Lifestyle Award recognizes students who perform 60 minutes of daily physical activity on five days per week for six of eight weeks while also adhering to weekly healthy eating guidelines.

The FitnessGram Scientific Advisory Board does not specifically endorse award programs focused on achieving high levels of fitness. However, the health-related PYFP awards recognize students for meeting important standards for physical fitness and physical activity; therefore, these individual awards can be incorporated effectively into school-based educational programming. Even so, consideration should be given to alternative ways to recognize school-level progress. Furthermore, if individual awards are used, care should be taken when introducing, explaining, and distributing them in order to keep the focus on promoting long-term physical activity behaviors. For example, because a students' ability to achieve FitnessGram standards can be affected by genetic predisposition and the timing of maturation, recognition should focus not merely on achieving fitness but on the importance of engaging in physical activity. Youth who do not achieve the standards should be encouraged to be more active in order to increase their fitness levels into the Healthy Fitness Zone. Youth who do achieve the standards should be acknowledged for their achievement *and* be encouraged to continue participating in physical activity in order to maintain their fitness. Following these guidelines helps educators maximize learning and motivate students.

Structured testing and rewards are not recommended for children in kindergarten through grade 3 because such mechanisms put too much emphasis on performance; in addition, there are no health-related criteria for aerobic capacity for children under the age of 10. Instead, the emphasis at this age should be placed on enjoying activity and learning about fitness assessments. With this goal in mind, the PYFP Fitness Club provides an age-appropriate alternative to structured fitness testing that recognizes students who learn the proper technique for the FitnessGram test items.

Presidential Active Lifestyle Award

Administered by the President's Council on Fitness, Sports, and Nutrition (PCFSN), the Presidential Active Lifestyle Award (PALA+) challenge includes a process-based award as part of its recognition program. The PALA+ program challenges students to stay on track with their physical activity and healthy eating habits for six out of eight weeks. PALA+ encourages students to commit to 60 minutes of physical activity on five days per week and to adhere to weekly healthy eating goals. The challenge can be used either instead of or in addition to the Presidential Youth Fitness Award to promote interest and involvement in physical activity. Used properly, PALA+ helps provide the basis for sound education about essential fitness concepts and motivates students to become active and stay active for a lifetime.

KEY CONCEPTS

- Recognize the importance of physical activity during physical education; help children learn and strive to meet the guidelines for daily physical activity—that is, 60 minutes per day of moderate to vigorous activity.

- Develop understanding of the factors—predisposing, enabling, and reinforcing—that influence fitness in order to design physical activities that are developmentally appropriate and motivating.

- Use the youth physical activity promotion model to bridge the gap between theory and application by providing students with regular feedback, encouraging them to set both short- and long-term goals, and teaching them the distinction between process and product goals.

- Use effective reinforcement in activity programs to pursue the ultimate goal of helping students increase their intrinsic motivation to be physically active.

- Give students the opportunity to set goals and increase their awareness of process-based awards (e.g., Presidential Active Lifestyle Award).

Communicating With Stakeholders

This chapter provides physical education teachers with communication strategies for sharing assessment and test-administration information with students, parents, faculty and staff members, administrators, and the community. Communicating a clear, consistent message to these key stakeholders is critical to the success of fitness education, and key communication opportunities are provided by the process of FitnessGram administration and assessment. Indeed, strategic communication should be used throughout fitness education to help stakeholders understand the importance of the *process* of fitness rather than just the scores.

In addition, effective communicators have the opportunity to engage stakeholders in their respective roles in supporting youth fitness. Stakeholders each play a defined role in youth fitness, which does not begin and end with physical education. To the contrary, it takes a collabora-

tive effort from all stakeholders to help youth be physically active and fit. As you review the many strategies presented in this chapter, please remain aware that no single strategy should be considered better than another. Rather, the chapter is designed to help physical education teachers communicate with and engage each stakeholder in the fitness education process. This engagement, in turn, can provide teachers with support and resources and solidify the team of stakeholders to advocate for youth fitness.

A conceptual framework for this approach—in which each stakeholder plays a role in the fitness education process—is provided in the social ecological model presented in chapter 3 (figure 3.1). The most integral role in this model is that of the physical educator, who has the unique opportunity to serve as the liaison between all stakeholders and facilitate connections between them.

STRATEGIES FOR COMMUNICATING THE FITNESS EDUCATION PROCESS

Over the years, physical education teachers have served effectively in their role as liaison in the fitness education process by making use of key resources and strategies. This section addresses many resources and strategies designed to help physical educators engage each stakeholder in understanding his or her unique role in the fitness education process. Table 4.1 provides sample strategies for communicating the fitness education process to all stakeholders; it also suggests a time frame for engaging each stakeholder.

Many people labor under misconceptions about the fitness education process and the purposes for which fitness data should be used. To improve understanding, physical educators can share resources with stakeholders to debunk myths—for example, the notion that fitness scores should be used for grading students or for evaluating teachers, physical education programs, or schools. In a nutshell, physical educators should clearly articulate the importance of approaching fitness not as a product but as a process.

Physical education teachers can support stakeholders by providing them with information that aids their understanding and advocates for appropriate uses of fitness scores. For example, if a student has not met the Healthy Fitness Zone (HFZ) for aerobic capacity, then she or he should be made aware of the score and helped to set goals to improve in this area. Parents should also be made aware of their child's fitness level and should provide support for the child's efforts to reach his or her individual goals. In the example just mentioned, the parent and child might decide to take brisk evening walks or jogs.

Table 4.1 Strategies for Communicating the Fitness Education Process

	Step 1: fitness concepts	Step 2: student preparation	Step 3: practice procedures	Step 4: assessment	Step 5: program planning and goal setting	Step 6: promoting and tracking physical activity	Step 7: reassessment	Step 8: revision and refinement of goals
Student	Instruction about fitness concepts	Preconditioning and practice for the assessment	Instruction about test items	Assessment of fitness levels	Fitness program planning, goal setting	• Promotion and tracking of physical activity • Use of ActivityGram and Activity Log	Reassessment	Revision of fitness program and goals
Parent	• Parent letter explaining components of fitness and test items • Information shared on school website and at parent meetings		• Reminder to parents of fitness assessment schedule • Distribution of parent report	• Parent review of report • Communication with parents about student goals		• Reminder to parents of fitness assessment schedule • Distribution of student report	• Parent review of report • Communication with parents about student goals

Faculty or staff member	• Incorporation of at least 30 minutes of physical activity for all students throughout the school day
	• Provision of ways to integrate fitness concepts in the classroom—for example:
	  • Language arts: writing to reflect on achievement of goals
	  • Mathematics: use of pedometers to see how many steps the class can total in a week
	  • Science: examination of the physiological effects of each health-related component of fitness
	  • Social studies: exploration of ways in which various cultures participate in physical activity
							Provision of motivational messaging from other faculty and staff about staying physically active

Administrator	Sharing of resources about the importance of healthy fitness levels	Invitations to visit class during fitness test administration	Provision of motivational messaging by administrator about staying physically active	Invitation to join students in tracking physical activity		Invitation to visit class during fitness test administration	Provision of motivational messaging from administrator about staying physically active
Community	Providing local media with information about how fitness assessment can benefit youth	Gaining support of community partners by hosting a health or fitness event (e.g., Day of Fitness, 5K walk/run)					

School faculty and administrators should also be attentive in providing the child with opportunities to be physically active each day during school. In addition, opportunities to be physically active *after* school can be provided by community organizations such as the YMCA, the local Boys and Girls Club, and local parks and recreation programs. This comprehensive approach, facilitated by the physical educator, provides the child with multiple opportunities and examples of ways to be physically active.

COMMUNICATING WITH STUDENTS

It is extremely important that students understand why they are taking part in the FitnessGram assessment. This understanding entails teaching what the FitnessGram assessment measures and why it holds value. Knowledge of the benefits of fitness (or negative consequences of a lack of fitness) associated with particular aspects of fitness is just as important as the score received in the assessment. Educators can find excellent activities for helping children learn health-related fitness concepts in the Physical Best activity guides offered by SHAPE America (2011a, 2011b).

Students also need to be taught the proper protocols for each assessment. To account for the fact that students learn in many different ways, physical education teachers should do the following for each assessment item.

1. Read through each protocol according to the manual.
2. Show a proper live demonstration or show the video provided in the web resource.
3. Have each student practice the protocol for each assessment prior to the day of the assessment.
4. On test day prior to beginning the assessment, take time to review the protocol to ensure proper form and technique for each assessment.

During the assessment, students may become anxious for a variety of reasons. For instance, they may feel nervous because they are participating in an assessment or because other students are watching them perform. They may also feel stressed if they know that they are unable to meet the Healthy Fitness Zone or if they have had a negative experience with fitness testing. Physical education teachers must be mindful of such concerns when assessing each student; here are some guidelines.

- Provide a safe location for students to perform the assessment.
- Never have the whole class or even a few students watch one student perform the assessment unless the student volunteers to provide a demonstration.
- Never post fitness scores for students to compare.
- Never use a fitness score as a grade.

When students complete a fitness assessment in a particular component, they should be reminded of the meaning of the assessment score; that is, all students should be taught how their score relates to their fitness level. Fortunately, fitness education provides an opportunity for teachers to help students go beyond the score. Specifically, this is the critical time to set goals and use ActivityGram and ActivityLog to help students work toward their goals and keep accurate logs or journals of their fitness routines. After a period of time for training, students should then have the opportunity to perform the assessment again as a measure of improvement, and their goals should be revised as necessary on an ongoing basis. Upon graduation, students should have learned to assess their own fitness, analyze the data, develop fitness plans, and, ultimately, motivate themselves to remain physically active for a lifetime (SHAPE America 2014).

Fitness assessment can also provide creative opportunities outside of physical education. For example, students might write an article for the school newspaper promoting fitness or create a video to be aired during the morning announcements exploring the benefits of healthy eating. Of course, the ultimate objective of a physical education program is to teach students the physical and behavioral skills necessary to be physically active for life. Communicating this message in a wide variety of ways is the best way for students to develop the knowledge, skills, and dispositions for success.

According to a position statement issued by the National Association for Sport and Physical Education (NASPE, now part of SHAPE America), students should not be graded on the basis of their fitness level (SHAPE America 2009). Physical education

HOW TO APPLY

teachers can, however, provide grades for students in many other areas related to fitness. Here are three options to consider:

- Quizzing students (e.g., giving knowledge tests) about cognitive concepts associated with health-related fitness
- Setting appropriate goals after reviewing the fitness score for each component of fitness
- Having students keep an activity log for a set period of time (e.g., through ActivityLog)

COMMUNICATING WITH PARENTS

It is impossible to overstate the importance of communicating effectively with parents. Physical education teachers must do more than simply provide parents with their child's fitness scores in a report; they must also communicate with parents throughout the fitness education process. Specifically, a parent should know *why* his or her child participates in fitness assessment, *what* the assessment entails and measures, and *how* to help the child improve or maintain his or her fitness. This proactive approach demands that teachers communicate with parents before, during, and after the fitness assessment. Keeping parents informed throughout the process may proactively address questions that would arise as the students participate in the fitness assessment.

Of course, because teachers carry many responsibilities, they are unlikely to be able to speak to the parents of each child individually at every stage of the fitness education process. They can, however, provide parents with FitnessGram information in various ways (in addition to parent meetings), such as by sending out letters and e-mails or posting the information on the school website. Most important, parents need to know that their children are cared for during the process of fitness assessment; to put it more directly, they should be assured that at no time will children be ostracized, embarrassed, or teased. They should also be assured that the FitnessGram philosophy calls for keeping scores private and using them not for grading purposes but for setting goals in order to improve or maintain appropriate fitness.

Communicating with parents is an ongoing process that teachers can accomplish in a variety of ways. Here are some examples.

- Provide parents with an informative letter at the beginning of the year.
- Provide links on the school or district website to the FitnessGram website and the parent resource guide found on the Presidential Youth Fitness Program website.
- Share the FitnessGram Student Report containing the results of the fitness assessment with parents.
- Hold a parent night in which students take parents through the fitness assessments; this approach can really help parents understand

Communicating About FitnessGram to Students, Parents, Administrators, and the Community
Spotlight on FitnessGram and ActivityGram

Mary Driemeyer
Physical Education Teacher
Lindbergh School District, St. Louis, Missouri

We work hard to ensure proper communication with, and awareness among, students, parents, administrators, and the community. With our students, we emphasize why fitness testing is conducted and give them an opportunity to practice and familiarize themselves with FitnessGram prior to testing. The reports have really helped open a line of communication between teachers, students, and parents. We also send a letter home to parents before testing to inform them of the dates and information that will be collected during the fitness assessment. We also use FitnessGram data for goal setting, and parents are now supporting students at home to help them progress toward reaching their goals. In addition, we work to get staff and administrators involved in supporting the testing and helping students with data entry into the FitnessGram software. FitnessGram scores also allow us to generate quick updates regarding progress of student groups toward program goals. Such updates provide the opportunity to highlight physical education program activities that have contributed to that progress.

the purpose of the assessments and how each assessment is performed.

- Provide periodic newsletters (hard-copy or electronic) to remind parents of the purpose of the fitness education process.
- Provide resources that teach parents how to engage their children in a positive manner with regard to physical activity. For example, you might provide information about youth sport, tips for being physically active as a family, or ways to positively reinforce a child by providing opportunities to participate in special physical activities.

COMMUNICATING WITH FACULTY AND STAFF

At any given school, many people work together to affect children in a positive manner. This is certainly true of physical educators, who can find multiple ways to collaborate in the school setting, particularly in the area of fitness assessment. Specifically, physical educators can use thoughtful and detailed collaborative planning to serve as advocates who promote healthy fitness levels for children. In fact, physical educators should collaborate regularly with other faculty members and staff members; fortunately, much of what is taught in physical education can be easily translated into the general curriculum.

For example, if students are being assessed on the PACER test, the physical educator can work—before the assessment—in partnership with appropriate classroom teachers to teach related concepts, such as estimation of time, changes in heart rate, and calculation of target heart rate. On the day of the assessment, the physical educator can send a brief e-mail reminding teachers of the assessment and asking them to watch for signs of fatigued students afterward. Then, both the physical educator and the classroom teachers can follow up with key questions that allow students to think and learn across subject areas.

It is also the responsibility of physical educators to educate their peers about health-related fitness. John Ratey's book *SPARK* provides information on scientific studies confirming that healthy, active students make better learners. To take advantage of this fact, physical education teachers can provide physical activities for classroom teachers to incorporate into their teaching—for example, recess periods, games, quick power walks with students, and concept learning through movement.

COMMUNICATING WITH ADMINISTRATORS

Administrative support is crucial to the successful implementation of a fitness assessment. This support can involve various parties—for example, principal, district-level administrator, curriculum specialist, superintendent—and communication at this level can take place in a variety of ways. For starters, administrators should be invited to be part of the fitness assessment process. This invitation gives the physical educator an opportunity to advocate for the importance of physical activity in school; it also helps administrators understand their role in the fitness education process. For example, the physical education teacher might help an administrator create a motivational message for use during morning announcements, provide support at a school board meeting, or enforce appropriate recess practices. The teacher should also encourage administrators to include messages about nutrition, fitness, and overall health in school and district mission statements. In turn, administrators should allocate resources to support student fitness.

Physical education teachers should also equip administrators with the information they need in order to fulfill their role in the fitness education process. For example, rather than asking an administrator to take time to craft a letter about fitness testing, a physical educator can provide the administrator with an appropriate letter; doing so ensures clear and accurate messaging. In addition, many informative resources are available for physical educators to share with administrators when they are advocating for fitness. For example, SHAPE America offers papers on various pertinent topics, such as appropriate practices in physical education (SHAPE America 2009) and the role of physical education in educating the whole child (NASPE 2004). For a full listing, SHAPE America members may login and visit www.shapeamerica.org/standards/guidelines/peguidelines.cfm.

Last, physical educators should advocate for their programs. When good things are happening, administrators need to be informed. This communication might take the form, for example, of short videos, information about physical education program successes during morning announcements, invitations to administrators to participate in physical education for a day, or collaboration with other faculty members in cross-curricular activities. Every school is unique, and every physical education teacher should be proactive in helping administrators find ways to support fitness assessment.

COMMUNICATING WITH THE COMMUNITY

Physical educators have a unique opportunity to gain support from the community. At a time when physical inactivity is prevalent in many communities, physical educators can serve as liaisons between schools and communities. Specifically, physical education teachers can inform key community stakeholders of the importance of fitness and ways in which they can help children in their community maintain or increase their fitness levels. Teachers should be thoughtful in selecting community partners and should consider how those partners can best help in the fitness education process. Before engaging partners in the fitness assessment process, teachers should also consult school policy regarding the involvement of community volunteers in the classroom setting. Here are some examples of ways in which a physical education teacher might inform community members and engage them in appropriate roles in physical fitness programming, promotion, and assessment.

• **Development of reliable trainers.** When conducting assessments, physical educators can seek out assistance from institutions of higher education. Using trained students (undergraduate or graduate) or university faculty to assist with class management can reduce the number of days spent on the assessment process, thus freeing more time for helping students develop the skills, knowledge, and dispositions called for by the physical education curriculum. A physical education teacher might also seek help with class management from retired school faculty or coaches from the local recreation department. Although the physical educator must spend time training these volunteers in order to get reliable fitness scores, individuals from these groups have experience in working with children and are generally responsible people.

• **Community health fairs.** Physical educators can host or delegate students, parents, or teachers to host a community health event, which can take place either on or off of the school campus. The event might focus, for example, on fitness assessments (e.g., parents participating in FitnessGram with their students) or on physical activity (e.g., a 5K run). A community event is an excellent way to bring partners together to provide support, build capacity, and find resources for youth fitness.

• **Local news stories.** Physical education teachers can also work with local newspapers and news stations to promote fitness assessment. Physical educators should proactively communicate the importance of the fitness education process, as well as inappropriate and appropriate strategies and ways in which stakeholders can play a role in youth fitness. This approach can reach community members who are not engaged in the schools. As a result, it may garner support and resources and help establish a positive connection between the physical education teacher and the community. Teachers should be aware that any media coverage of students will require a media release from students' parents.

• **Partnering with organizations.** Many schools have "partners in education," or community organizations that partner with the school for a common purpose. For example, public health agencies, city parks and recreation departments, and local businesses all have a vested interest in youth health. In your efforts to teach the importance of youth fitness, these organizations can help by advocating for physical activity during school, helping secure joint-use agreements for facilities, and providing funding for initiatives geared toward youth fitness. Again, each school is unique, and physical education teachers should search for key partners that match the needs of their school.

KEY CONCEPTS

- The physical education teacher is the liaison (middle person) who communicates the responsibilities of each stakeholder throughout the fitness education process.

- As the liaison, the physical education teacher can help all stakeholders collaborate in a way that provides an optimum setting for children to improve their fitness or maintain healthy levels of fitness.

- The physical education teacher should adhere to the school's process for allowing outside personnel to help in the classroom setting.

PART II

FitnessGram Assessment Module

The FitnessGram assessment measures five components of physical fitness that are important to overall health and optimal function. The components are aerobic capacity, body composition, muscular strength, muscular endurance, and flexibility. For most areas, several test options are provided and one test item is recommended. Each item is scored using criterion-referenced standards based on the level of fitness needed for good health. Research and validation work conducted over many years have helped refine these standards so that we now have separate criteria for boys and girls at different ages. For specific information about FitnessGram standards, readers may access the *FitnessGram/ ActivityGram Reference Guide* (Plowman and Meredith 2013) online at www.cooperinstitute.org/ reference-guide. Because only modest amounts of activity are needed to obtain health benefits, most students who perform regular physical activity should be able to achieve a score that places them either in or above the Healthy Fitness Zone (HFZ) on all FitnessGram test items.

Chapter 5 covers general principles for conducting fitness testing, guidelines for testing primary students, and general guidelines for safety. Chapters 6, 7, and 8 provide detailed information, respectively, about assessing aerobic capacity, body composition, and musculoskeletal fitness. A number of the assessments require certain equipment, and the web resource includes information about sources of equipment and instructions for constructing homemade equipment (see figure).

One important feature of the FitnessGram assessment is the inclusion of a physical activity assessment. Although fitness itself is important, it cannot be maintained unless children are physically active. With this reality in mind, the physical activity assessment includes three questions that help customize feedback for the individual student reports; these questions are addressed in detail in chapter 9, which also provides alternative suggestions for teachers without access to the FitnessGram software. Chapters 10 and 11 focus on interpreting FitnessGram test results and making effective use of the data.

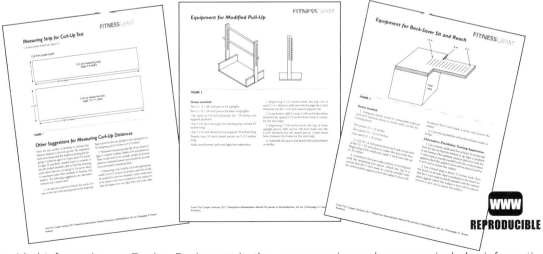

The section titled Information on Testing Equipment in the accompanying web resource includes information about where to purchase equipment, as well as building plans for constructing some equipment on your own.

FitnessGram Test Administration

When conducting the FitnessGram assessment, efficiency depends on appropriate preparation. The sheer amount of time required to conduct FitnessGram testing also depends on the test items you use, the number of students being tested, and the number of volunteers assisting you. To facilitate efficient test administration, the accompanying web resource includes individual and class score sheets (see figure 5.1, a–c), as well as Healthy Fitness Zone standards charts (figure 5.2, a and b) for use in evaluating student performance. Having established these basics, this chapter presents key considerations for administering and scoring fitness-test items.

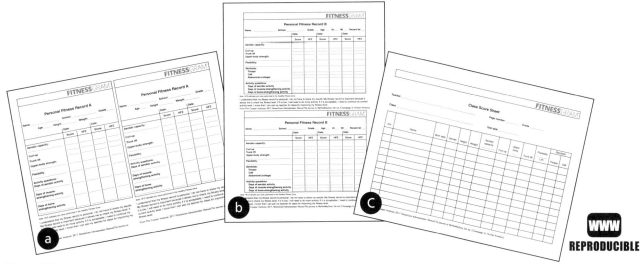

Figure 5.1 Score sheets available in the accompanying web resource include (a) Personal Fitness Record A, (b) Personal Fitness Record B, and (c) Class Score Sheet.

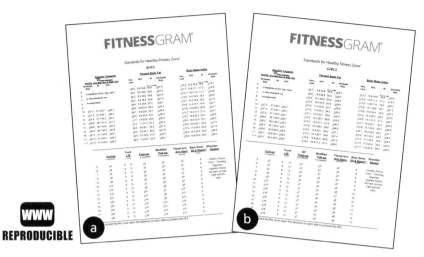

Figure 5.2   The Healthy Fitness Zone standards charts for *(a)* boys and *(b)* girls are available in the accompanying web resource.

IMPORTANCE OF RELIABLE SCORES

Fitness can be difficult to assess with high reliability. Even so, given the program implications of fitness data (whether positive or negative), physical education teachers should take a variety of practical steps to minimize measurement error, including the following (Morrow et al. 2016):

1. Attain adequate knowledge of test descriptions.

2. Give proper demonstrations and instructions.

3. Develop good student and teacher preparation through adequate practice trials.

4. Conduct reliability studies.

Although fitness assessments should focus on educating and increasing awareness, it is also our responsibility as physical educators to ensure that student data are valid and reliable. Producing consistent, accurate, and valid FitnessGram data empowers students to develop lifelong healthy habits.

CONSIDERATIONS FOR TESTING IN THE PRIMARY GRADES

When testing children in grades K through 3, focus on encouraging students and instructing them in proper technique. Aerobic capacity standards are not recommended for children under the age of 10. In order to create the best instructional environment

Strategies for Gathering Consistent and Reliable Data

Spotlight on FitnessGram and ActivityGram

Jill Camron

Oversight of Categorical Programs: SUHSD Physical Education
Salinas Union High School District, Salinas, California

The Salinas Union High School District continues to improve its FitnessGram scores through a variety of methods. For one thing, district-level trainings are conducted for all physical educators to address how to properly proctor and administer each of the FitnessGram test options. Teachers may then give students the opportunity to select specific test items for each of the list of options that they would like to include in their personal assessment. Schools also collaborate to create game plans for preparing students throughout the year for FitnessGram testing. In addition, the district supports schools by providing appropriate equipment for administering FitnessGram, such as modified pull-up systems, curl-up mats, sit-and-reach boxes, and pulse analyzers. We also display posters indicating the Healthy Fitness Zone standards and sample FitnessGram reports in school locker rooms throughout the district.

Our district has used FitnessGram for several years and the program has increased our communication with parents and students. After the first year, we saw a 5 percent increase in the number of students passing five of six FitnessGram tests at the middle school level and a 7 percent increase at the high school level.

Emphasis on Teaching—Not Testing—in the Primary Grades

Spotlight on FitnessGram and ActivityGram

Joanna Faerber
Instructor of Physical Education
University Laboratory School, Baton Rouge, Louisiana

University Laboratory School is a K-12 public school located on the campus of Louisiana State University as part of the College of Human Sciences and Education. Part of our physical education curriculum involves FitnessGram. When assessing grades K through 3, we emphasize not the physical results but the process of learning about fitness components and having fun. Making fitness testing fun at an early age helps create a positive association for years to come.

for all students in a class, aerobic capacity standards for 10-year-olds are used in the FitnessGram software for students who are 9 years old but in grade 4. Although the standards for students in grades K through 3 are provided for other test items, we greatly discourage focusing on performance with these children.

CONSIDERATIONS FOR TESTING IN THE SECONDARY GRADES

Participation in all types of physical activity tends to decline as students age. Physical activity levels are also influenced by other biological factors (e.g., sex, race), as well as sociological and environmental factors (U.S. Department of Health and Human Services 1996). Therefore, it is important to create a testing environment that motivates and empowers students to try their best on the FitnessGram items. This goal can be achieved by using a variety of teaching strategies, such as self-assessment, student goal setting, portfolios, and personal-best testing. Before testing, ensure that students understand the five health-related fitness components—aerobic capacity, muscular strength, muscular endurance, flexibility, and body composition—and how they relate to individual health.

CONSIDERATIONS FOR SAFETY

FitnessGram test items have been administered to millions of students and have been shown to be very safe. Even so, incidents can occur during any strenuous activity; therefore, we must take appropriate precautions. Before administering any FitnessGram test item, make sure that you are aware of all of your students' health conditions. Most schools and districts have established policies related to medical information, medical records, and medical clearance for activity. If you are unfamiliar with these policies or with your students' medical information, meet with your school nurse, principal, or other personnel who can provide you with the needed information to follow relevant protocols. For example, a child with a cardiovascular condition may require special consideration during the aerobic capacity test. In all cases, the primary objective should be to maximize student safety.

Students should also be conditioned adequately before taking a test. In addition, as with other strenuous activities, always consider children's safety when testing in a hot climate. Specifically, make sure that children are adequately hydrated and conditioned and notify the school nurse of FitnessGram testing dates.

TESTING IN LARGE GROUPS OR CLASSES

Prior to testing, ensure that students understand the purpose of the testing, the importance of health-related fitness, and its effects on a person's health. You can also help students understand the purpose of testing by showing FitnessGram protocol videos and administering cognitive tests.

When testing in large groups and classes, use the following guidelines:

HOW TO APPLY

- Communicate lesson goals and purposes before conducting the official test; ensure that all students understand why they are being tested.

- Make sure that you have enough equipment to keep all students active and engaged; if equipment is limited, set up stations to increase participation and decrease wait time.

- Check your environment to ensure that students have enough space to move without running into each other. Establish a positive testing environment that fosters maintaining personal results and does not encourage students to ask around class "How did you score?" Emphasize teamwork and social responsibility before testing. If students are working with partners, make certain that each student is working with someone he or she can trust to maintain the privacy of his results. Allowing students to select partners will help to ensure students are comfortable with testing each other.

- Before conducting official tests, practice with students to familiarize them with the testing protocols and how you plan to structure the test day.

- Review your safety policies and procedures with students.

- Maximize student participation in order to minimize off-task behavior.

- Use stations and small groups to keep everyone active and involved. FitnessGram cue cards (sold online by US Games) are a great way to remind students of specific test protocols and cues. If you are using the testing-stations strategy, determine which station you will supervise while students participate (for enjoyment) at other skill or fitness-related stations. Position yourself where you can supervise all students while attending closely to your designated station.

- To organize student results, use the Personal Fitness Record forms from the accompanying web resource (figure 5.1, *a* and *b*).

- If you use small groups, clearly define roles to help each student stay focused. For example, if students are in groups of three, one can perform the test while the second watches for form breaks and the third keeps count.

- Use paraprofessionals, parents, or community volunteers (e.g., nurses, college students, fitness center staff members) to help with classroom management. Increased adult supervision helps keep students motivated and on task. These individuals should be trained, and if time permits you can also take them through the stations, using the FitnessGram cue cards as reminders. Another way to train volunteers is to have them watch the test protocols provided in the web resource prior to the official testing day. Review form breaks and testing objectives with them.

- Structure your environment to limit transition times between activities or tests; for example, use music or another signal to communicate when it is time for students to rotate or switch roles.

- If you are not using small groups or stations but do have access to a paraprofessional or adult volunteer, consider dividing the class in half. In this approach, half of the students test in pairs or small groups in a designated area of the gym while the other half participates in a familiar activity that does not use the same fitness skills being tested that day. For example, do not use a tag game on the same day you conduct PACER testing because this type of game would create fatigue and perhaps cause the results to be low. Rotate groups once the test has been conducted. This technique keeps all students active, and those who are not testing are not just standing around watching those being tested.

TEST ITEMS

Table 5.1 shows the five areas of health-related fitness assessed by FitnessGram and the test items for each area. FitnessGram test items are selected to assess not skill or agility but important aspects of a student's health-related fitness.

CONSIDERATIONS FOR TESTING STUDENTS WITH DISABILITIES

In many situations, you will work with students with disabilities who are either unable to complete the FitnessGram assessment or are able to complete it but only in a way that results in scores that cannot be evaluated fairly in terms of the Healthy Fitness Zone standards. Nonetheless, when certain physical fitness components are deemed important in education, they are equally important for all students. However, because FitnessGram was developed to assess physical fitness in children and youth without disabilities, it may not be the most appropriate assessment for children with disabilities. At the same time, the need for physical fitness assessment exists in all youth populations, and many classes today include students of all ability levels; therefore, teachers need to develop understanding of fitness assessment for students with disabilities.

The presence of a disability should not exclude a student from participation in a FitnessGram assessment; however, if it is determined that proper FitnessGram protocol cannot be followed, then alternative strategies or assessments must be implemented. We suggest that teachers needing assistance with modified assessment protocols consult the *Brockport Physical Fitness Test Manual* (Winnick and Short

Table 5.1 FitnessGram Test Items

Component of health-related fitness	Definition	Test
Aerobic capacity	Body's ability to take in, transport, and use O_2 to convert fuel to energy during exercise	• PACER • One-mile run • Walk test
Muscular strength	Ability of muscles to exert force	• Modified pull-up
Muscular endurance	Ability of muscles to contract repeatedly	• 90 degree push-up • Flexed arm hang • Curl-up • Trunk lift
Flexibility	Range of motion at a joint	• Back-saver sit and reach • Shoulder stretch

Body composition	Appropriateness of weight relative to height (body mass index); level of fat mass in the body (percent body fat)	• Body mass index (height and weight)
		• Body fat percentage
		   • Skinfold measurement
		   • Bioelectrical impedance analysis

2014), which provides Adapted Fitness Zones (AFZs), as well as guidance for determining how students with disabilities can be assessed in some instances with the Healthy Fitness Zone standards. For youth who do not participate in any assessment, we suggest monitoring physical activity through a tool such as ActivityGram Lite (Youth Activity Profile), which is included in the FitnessGram software, as well as programs such PALA+ (discussed in chapter 3).

In addition, some students are physically capable of performing FitnessGram tests but have attention or behavioral issues that prevent or limit their completion of certain test items. For such students, other strategies can be implemented in the classroom to increase their potential for following FitnessGram protocols:

- Consider collaborating with the student's para-educator or paraprofessional to develop strategies for increasing attention span and time on task and addressing other behavioral management factors.

- Be flexible and open to assessing students in settings outside of the main gym area that may be less stimulating and more accommodating (e.g., quiet hallway, empty classroom, corner of the gym).

- Evaluate the student's behavior on the day of testing; if negative behaviors cannot be sufficiently managed, consider conducting the assessment on another day rather than giving no credit for the affected test items.

- Consider whether to seek assistance through special education teachers, peer tutors, or other reverse-inclusion techniques.

- Find out whether the student has an Individual Education Plan (IEP) for physical education or a behavior intervention plan. If so, review the plan for reinforcement or behavior management strategies that may be useful during fitness testing.

Additional Resources

The Presidential Youth Fitness Program offers free Brockport assessment resources on its website (www.pyfp.org). The *Brockport Physical Fitness Test Manual* can be ordered from Human Kinetics at www.HumanKinetics.com.

EXEMPTIONS FOR STUDENTS

FitnessGram software allows administrators to use a coding system to note which students were not tested or were tested partially for a FitnessGram test event. These exemptions are determined solely by the user in order to document such cases. Exemptions might be made, for example, due to absence, injury, disability, parental opt-out, or the student no longer being in the class. A student can be permanently exempted for all test events or may be exempted per test item for any specific test event. For information about how to set up exemptions, please review the user guides in the FitnessGram software. Teachers without access to the software should note any exemptions in the affected student's Personal Fitness Record.

Strategies for Testing Students With Disabilities
Spotlight on FitnessGram and ActivityGram

Linda C. Hilgenbrinck, PhD, CAPE
Adapted Physical Education Specialist
Denton I.S.D., Denton, TX

In Denton I.S.D., our goal is to ensure that each student with disability who is unable to participate in the entire FitnessGram assessment be given as much of the test as is feasible. Because the test is state-mandated in Texas, the Individualized Education Program team discusses any needed modifications or alternative testing as recommended by highly qualified specialists in adapted physical education.

In working with these students, we use a customized FitnessGram Score Sheet developed specifically to reflect testing variations and accommodations made for students with disability. Enabling our students to participate in testing in their own best way, and as safely as possible, is one way of helping them be fully included rather than separate from their same-age peers.

More generally, our teachers use a variety of creative activities to educate students about the importance of fitness. Before testing, students are educated about the "FitnessGram way" of performing the fitness items in order to assure proper form. This education begins the process of making fitness an individual responsibility for each student to perform as regularly as possible.

As an adapted physical education teacher, I extend the general physical educator's teaching on all FitnessGram test items. I routinely have my students perform the test items as best they can. Students who do not need modifications perform and practice the item as it will be done on the day of testing. For students who need modifications, appropriate alternative activities are used to help each student improve his or her strength and flexibility and learn the desired movement.

So much of what we do must be individualized in order to truly meet students' needs. We address individualization through teaching strategies and differentiated instruction as is appropriate for each student.

KEY CONCEPTS

- Although fitness assessments should focus on educating and on increasing awareness, it is also an educator's responsibility to ensure that student data are valid and secure (in compliance with federal and state privacy laws).

- Testing for children in grades K through 3 should focus on encouragement and instruction in proper technique. Aerobic capacity standards are available for children 10 years or older, and students who are in grade 4 but are 9 years old may be evaluated using the standards for 10-year-olds.

- Student safety should always be a priority. Ensure that you are aware of students' health conditions and that you are familiar with school and district policies related to medical information, records, and clearance for activity.

- Adjust your test administration strategies based on class size and age group. Using best practices gives your students the best opportunity to have a positive experience and gives you the best likelihood of obtaining valid and reliable data.

- When performing fitness assessments for students with disabilities, many FitnessGram test items may be appropriate. However, if proper protocol cannot be followed, consider options for alternative testing (e.g., the Brockport Physical Fitness Test).

Aerobic Capacity

Perhaps the most important aspect of any fitness program is aerobic capacity. Research clearly indicates that adequate levels of aerobic capacity are associated with reduced risk of all-cause mortality, high blood pressure, coronary heart disease, obesity, diabetes, some forms of cancer, and other health problems in adults (Blair et al. 1989) and clinical risk factors for cardiovascular disease and metabolic syndrome in children and adolescents. The evidence documenting the health benefits of physical activity has been well described, and this information provides the basis for U.S. physical activity guidelines (HHS 2008).

Aerobic capacity is the maximum amount of oxygen that the body is able to use to perform work. The best measure of aerobic capacity is generally considered to be a laboratory measurement of maximal oxygen uptake ($\dot{V}O_2$max). Because oxygen uptake can be influenced by body size, aerobic capacity is typically expressed in relation to body weight—that is, in terms of milliliters of O_2 consumed per kilogram of body weight per minute, or $ml \cdot kg^{-1} \cdot min^{-1}$.

The term *aerobic capacity* is often used interchangeably with other terms, such as *cardiovascular fitness, cardio, aerobics,* and *endurance.* However, though these terms do refer to the body's ability to use oxygen, *aerobic capacity* refers specifically to the maximum amount that can be used by the body. Similarly, many terms have been used to describe

this dimension of physical fitness, including the following: cardiovascular fitness, cardiorespiratory fitness, cardiorespiratory endurance, aerobic fitness, aerobic work capacity, and physical working capacity. Although defined somewhat differently, these terms can generally be considered synonymous with *aerobic capacity.* Here is a brief indication of typical usage of four terms often used along with, or in relation to, aerobic capacity:

- *Aerobic fitness* is often used to describe the body's ability to use oxygen to create energy.
- *Cardiorespiratory endurance* is often used to describe the ability to sustain exercise that increases heart rate and breathing rate (e.g., running, cycling, swimming, cross-country skiing).
- *Cardiovascular fitness* is often used to describe the body's ability to use oxygen to create energy.
- *Endurance* is often used to describe the ability to perform exercise for an extended period of time.

The FitnessGram test battery provides three field tests of aerobic capacity: the PACER, the one-mile run, and the walk test. Estimates of aerobic capacity are reported in terms of $\dot{V}O_2$max and expressed in the form of $ml \cdot kg^{-1} \cdot min^{-1}$. In addition, for the one-mile run and the walk test, calculation of aerobic capacity requires the use of body mass index (BMI), which is calculated from height and weight. Therefore, when the FitnessGram software is used with the one-mile run and the walk test, height and weight must be entered in order to estimate $\dot{V}O_2$max. Accurate estimates of measured $\dot{V}O_2$max and high test–retest reliability have been demonstrated for all three FitnessGram measures of aerobic capacity (PACER, one-mile run, and walk test).

The following sections provide guidelines for administering and scoring all three tests. For additional information about the aerobic capacity assessments, see the *FitnessGram/ActivityGram Reference Guide* (Plowman and Meredith 2013), which can be downloaded at www.cooperinstitute.org/reference-guide.

OVERVIEW OF FITNESSGRAM STANDARDS FOR AEROBIC CAPACITY

The FitnessGram Scientific Advisory Board has worked to ensure that all of the assessments are scored using health-related standards. It has been possible to develop objective health standards for aerobic fitness expressed as $\dot{V}O_2$max thanks to nationally representative fitness data provided by the National Health and Nutrition Examination Survey (NHANES) between 1999 and 2002. Detailed information about the development of the standards is provided in the *FitnessGram/ActivityGram Reference Guide* (Plowman and Meredith 2013) and in a comprehensive research supplement published in the *American Journal of Preventive Medicine* (Morrow, Going, and Welk 2011). For now, here are some key points about the aerobic fitness standards:

1. Regardless of the assessment used, estimates of aerobic capacity are expressed in terms of $\dot{V}O_2$max and in the form of ml·kg^{-1}·min^{-1}. $\dot{V}O_2$max is estimated from equations developed specifically for the PACER or one-mile run. When using the FitnessGram software to report results, estimation of $\dot{V}O_2$max requires entry of the following data: for the one-mile run, performance time, age, sex, height, and weight; for the PACER, laps completed, age, and sex. Teachers not using the Fitness-Gram software can access the online FitnessGram Score Sheet calculator spreadsheet, which can be downloaded at www.pyfp.org.

2. The health-related standards used to evaluate aerobic capacity are age- and sex-specific and also take into account typical changes during growth and maturation. As a result, the values for boys increase with age, whereas the values for girls decrease with age. These changes do not, however, imply higher expectations for boys and lower expectations for girls; rather, they are reflective of the natural developmental trends for boys and girls (i.e., boys gain muscle with age, whereas girls tend to gain body fat through adolescence). Therefore, the lines reflect the same relative level of fitness across age for boys and girls.

3. The FitnessGram standards released in 2010 are equivalent for 10- and 11-year-old boys and girls. From a developmental perspective, boys and girls at these young ages are more similar than different. As they mature, however, boys and girls follow different developmental trends, so the fitness standards follow these tracks (similar for young children and different as children mature).

4. The 2010 standards allow classification into three distinct zones: Healthy Fitness, Needs Improvement, and Needs Improvement—Health Risk. These three zones are shown for boys and for girls in figure 6.1. Students whose scores are above the top line for their sex are classified in the Healthy Fitness Zone, meaning that they possess sufficient fitness for good health. Students whose score falls between the two lines for their sex are classified in the Needs Improvement Zone and receive a message that they should work to reach the Healthy Fitness Zone. Students whose scores fall below the bottom line for their sex are classified in the Needs Improvement—Health Risk Zone. This

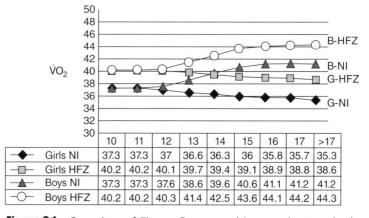

Comparison of Boys and Girls

	10	11	12	13	14	15	16	17	>17
◆ Girls NI	37.3	37.3	37	36.6	36.3	36	35.8	35.7	35.3
■ Girls HFZ	40.2	40.2	40.1	39.7	39.4	39.1	38.9	38.8	38.6
▲ Boys NI	37.3	37.3	37.6	38.6	39.6	40.6	41.1	41.2	41.2
○ Boys HFZ	40.2	40.2	40.3	41.4	42.5	43.6	44.1	44.2	44.3

Figure 6.1 Overview of FitnessGram aerobic capacity standards: comparison of boys and girls.

lowest fitness zone provides youth and parents with an appropriate warning that the child's low level of fitness increases health risks. Thus the use of these three distinct fitness zones makes it possible to provide specific information to children and parents about individual health and potential health risks.

Progressive Aerobic Cardiovascular Endurance Run (PACER)

Recommended

The PACER (Progressive Aerobic Cardiovascular Endurance Run) is a multistage fitness test adapted from the 20-meter shuttle-run test published by Leger and Lambert in 1982 and revised in 1988 (Leger et al.). The test is progressive in intensity; in other words, it is easy at the beginning but gets harder. The progressive nature of the test provides a built-in warm-up and helps children pace themselves effectively. The test has been set to music to create a valid, fun alternative to the customary distance-run test for measuring aerobic capacity. The music and the audio pacing for the test are available in the accompanying web resource.

The PACER is recommended for all ages, but its use is *strongly* recommended for students in the primary grades. It is recommended for a number of reasons, including the following:

- All students are more likely to have a positive experience in performing the PACER than with other aerobic capacity test items.
- The PACER helps students learn the skill of pacing.
- Students who have a poorer performance will finish first and therefore will not be subjected to the embarrassment of being the last person to complete the test.

When you administer the test with primary children, place emphasis on allowing the children to have a good time while learning how to take the test and how to pace themselves. Allow children to continue to run as long as they wish and as long as they are still enjoying the activity. The main goal for young children is to give them the opportunity to experience the assessment and enjoy it.

Test Objective

The objective of the PACER test is to run as long as possible with continuous movement back and forth across a 20-meter space at a specified pace that gets faster with each passing minute. A 15-meter version has also been developed for teachers with smaller facilities.

Equipment and Facilities

Administering the PACER requires a flat, nonslippery surface at least 20 meters long; if you do not have adequate indoor space, you can use an outdoor area. Designate a specific area for finished runners and scorekeepers. Plan for each runner to have a running space that is 40 to 60 inches (1.02 to 1.52 meters) wide and consider painting or drawing lines to help students run in a straight line. Students should wear nonslip shoes. The PACER also requires you to have a computer, laptop, or handheld music device (e.g., MP3 player) connected to speakers with adequate volume; a measuring tape; marker cones; a pencil; and appropriate score sheets (20-meter or 15-meter) (figure 6.2, *a–d*).

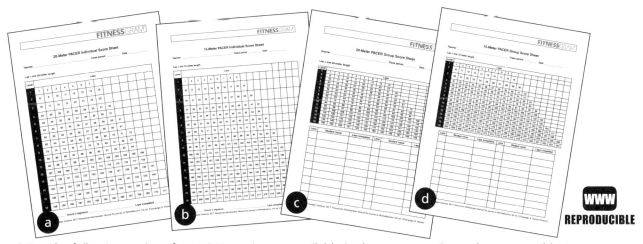

Figure 6.2 The following options for PACER scoring are available in the accompanying web resource: *(a)* 20-meter PACER Individual Score Sheet, *(b)* 15-meter PACER Individual Score Sheet, *(c)* 20-meter PACER Group Score Sheet, and *(d)* 15-meter PACER Group Score Sheet.

Because many gyms are not 20 meters long, an alternate PACER music track is included in the accompanying web resource for use with the 15-meter version of the test. The procedures described in the following instructions are the same for the 15-meter distance, but the alternate music track and scoring sheet are required to track the number of laps. The 15-meter PACER test is designed for use only in elementary schools where the gymnasium is not of adequate length to accommodate the 20-meter version.

Test Instructions

1. Select and download the desired PACER cadence in the accompanying web resource.

2. Before test day, allow students to listen to several minutes of PACER music from the accompanying web resource so that they know what to expect. Students should then be allowed at least two practice sessions.

3. Make copies of the appropriate PACER score sheet for each group of students to be tested. The PACER Individual Score Sheet is used when students or other scorers are counting laps for individual participants. If, on the other hand, you are scoring a group of students at one time, use the PACER Group Score Sheet.

4. Mark the course with marker cones to indicate lanes and use a tape or chalk line at each end. A schematic PACER diagram is presented in figure 6.3.

5. Allow students to select a partner. Have students who are being tested line up behind the start line. Partners who are counting laps should sit in a designated space.

6. Each student being tested should run across the full marked distance and cross the line with both feet by the time the next tone sounds. At the sound of the tone, each student turns around and runs back to the other end. If a student gets to the line before the tone, she or he must wait for the tone before running in the other direction. Each student continues in this manner until he or she fails twice to reach the line before the tone.

7. A tone sounds at the end of the time allowed for each lap, and a different tone sounds at the end of each level. The different tone serves to indicate the end of the time allowed for that lap and also alerts runners that the pace will get faster. Inform students that when the different tone sounds, they should not stop but should continue the test by turning and running toward the other end of the area.

8. The first time that a student does not reach the line before the tone sounds, the student stops where he or she is and reverses direction immediately, attempting to get back on pace. This lap constitutes a form break but is counted as a complete lap. The test is considered complete as of the next time (i.e., the second time) the student fails to reach the line before the tone sounds. The two misses do not have to be consecutive; the test is over after two total misses. Upon completing the test, the student should continue to walk and then stretch in the designated cool-down area. Testing procedures are diagrammed in figure 6.3.

9. A student who remains at one end of the testing area through two tones (does not run to the other end and back) should be scored as having two misses; therefore, his or her test is over.

Scoring

In the PACER test, a lap consists of one 20-meter or 15-meter segment, which is the distance from one end of the course to the other. In other words, do *not* use a "down and back" count for the test. The scorer records lap numbers (crossing off each lap number as it is completed) on a PACER Individual Score Sheet (20-meter or 15-meter); thus the recorded score indicates the total number of laps completed by the student. Failing to cross the line before the tone occurs constitutes a form break. As with many other FitnessGram test items, the first form break is counted as a completion. Therefore, the PACER score consists of the number of laps completed prior to the second time the student does not get to the line before the tone.

The number of laps completed by a student is used with his or her age to estimate aerobic capacity. If using the FitnessGram software, simply enter the number of laps completed, and that number will be used to generate individualized feedback. Aerobic capacity can also be determined by referring to the PACER Lookup Charts included in the web resource (see figure 6.4).

Because criterion standards are not available for students aged 5 through 9 years (grades K through 3), aerobic capacity scores and feedback are not provided for these ages. For these younger students, the object of the test is simply to participate and begin learning how to take the test. The main goal is to provide these students with the opportunity to have a positive experience with the PACER assessment. Students who are 9 years old but in grade 4 can receive a score evaluated against the criterion standard for 10-year-old students; all 10-year-old students receive a score, regardless of grade level.

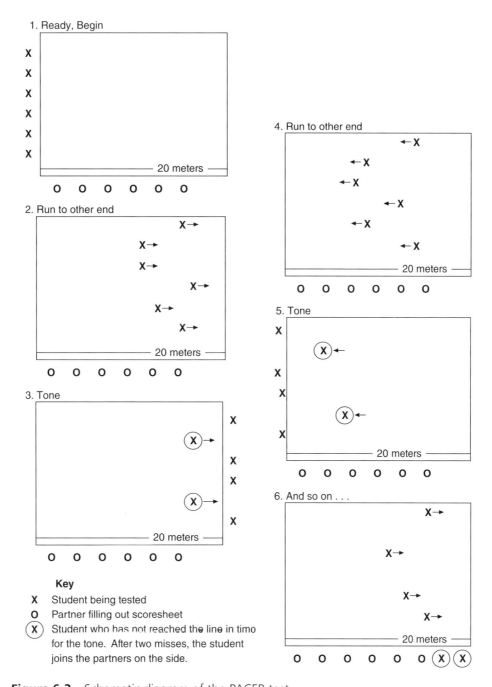

1. Ready, Begin
2. Run to other end
3. Tone
4. Run to other end
5. Tone
6. And so on . . .

Key
X Student being tested
O Partner filling out scoresheet
(X) Student who has not reached the line in time for the tone. After two misses, the student joins the partners on the side.

Figure 6.3 Schematic diagram of the PACER test.

Suggestions for Test Administration

- Both PACER audio tracks provided in the accompanying web resource contain 21 levels (1 level per minute for 21 minutes). During the first minute, the 20-meter version allows 9 seconds to run the distance, whereas the 15-meter version allows 6.75 seconds. The lap time decreases by about 0.5 second at each successive level. Before administering the test, allow students to practice it and help them understand that the speed increases with each minute.

- A tone indicates the end of a lap (one 20-meter or 15-meter distance). Students run from one end to the other between each set of tones. Caution students not to begin too fast; in fact, the beginning speed is very slow.

- A different tone at the end of each minute indicates both the end of a level and an increase in speed.

Students should be alerted that the speed will increase when they hear the different tone. Make clear to students that when they hear the different tone, they should turn around at the line and immediately continue running. Some students have a tendency to hesitate when they hear the different tone.

- A student who cannot reach the line before the tone sounds is given one chance to regain the pace. The second time the student cannot reach

the line before the tone, his or her test is considered complete.

- Groups of students may be tested at the same time. With this method, adult volunteers can be asked to help record scores; students can also record scores for each other (or for younger students).

- Each runner must be allowed a path that is 40 to 60 inches (1.02 to 1.52 meters) wide; it may work best to mark the course.

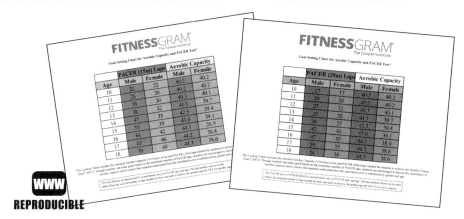

Figure 6.4 Instructors who do not use the FitnessGram software can use the PACER Lookup Charts, which are available in the accompanying web resource.

One-Mile Run

Alternative

The one-mile run can be used instead of the PACER to provide an estimate of aerobic capacity ($\dot{V}O_2$max), and it is a very good alternative assessment for students who enjoy running and are highly motivated. Scoring of the one-mile run requires the student's height and weight because the calculation of aerobic capacity includes BMI. For teachers who do not have access to the FitnessGram software, the FitnessGram Score Sheet calculator (spreadsheet) is available online at www.pyfp.org.

Test Objective

The objective of this assessment is to run one mile (1.61 kilometer) as fast as possible (i.e., in the shortest possible time). If a student gets tired, it is okay for him or her to walk if necessary, but students should be encouraged to try to maintain at least a slow jog throughout the assessment. The reason is that a walking pace is unlikely to enable the student to finish the mile in less than 13:01 minutes, which is the threshold for obtaining an aerobic capacity score because aerobic capacity cannot be accurately calculated for scores greater than 13 minutes. Therefore, students under the age of 13 years who cannot complete the one-mile run in less than 13 minutes should be allowed to do the PACER test. Students who are 13 years or older who cannot complete the one-mile run in less than 13 minutes should be allowed to do the PACER or the walk test.

Equipment and Facilities

This test requires a flat and accurately measured running course, as well as a stopwatch, a pencil, and appropriate score sheets (see figure 6.5). The course can consist of a track or any other measured area (whether measured by a tape measure or a cross country wheel). Caution: If the track is metric or is shorter than 440 yards, adjust the running course as needed (1 mile = 1,609.34 meters or 1,760 yards; 400 meters = 437.45 yards). For example, on a 400-meter track, the run should consist of four laps plus 10 yards.

Test Instructions

1. Describe the course to students and encourage them to try to complete the distance in the shortest possible time.
2. Remind students to listen for their time as they cross the line at the end of the one-mile distance.

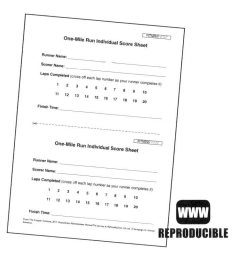

Figure 6.5 The score sheet for the one-mile run test is available in the accompanying web resource.

3. Many students begin too fast and tire out; remind students ahead of time to use appropriate pacing in order to get an accurate assessment.
4. To initiate the assessment, provide a signal, such as "Ready . . . start."
5. As students cross the finish line, their time should be called out, either to them or to their partners, then recorded.

Scoring

Scoring of the one-mile run is based on the total time, but this data point cannot be used to estimate aerobic capacity unless the child's age, sex, and BMI (obtained from height and weight) are also available in the data set. Teachers without access to the FitnessGram software should use the FitnessGram Score Sheet calculator (spreadsheet), which is available online at www.pyfp.org. If you use the spreadsheet, use the calculated $\dot{V}O_2$max score and the Healthy Fitness Zone standards chart provided in the web resource to determine how to classify the student's performance.

The one-mile run score consists of the time required to complete the distance. To calculate aerobic capacity for the one-mile run, enter the time in minutes and seconds into the software, which will estimate the child's aerobic capacity. The software then uses that capacity to determine the child's fitness zone and provide appropriate feedback.

Because criterion standards are not available for students in grades K through 3, aerobic capacity scores and feedback are not provided for these ages. For these younger students, the object of the test is simply to complete the one-mile distance at a comfortable pace and practice pacing; therefore, it is not necessary to time the run. Alternatively, the time for young students is just recorded in the software, but no performance standard is used to evaluate their score. Students who are 9 years old but in grade 4 receive a score evaluated against the standards for 10-year-old students; all 10-year-olds receive a score, regardless of grade level.

In addition to the one-mile performance time, each student's height and weight are also required in order to calculate his or her aerobic capacity. Calculation of aerobic capacity also requires a score of less than 13:01. Scores that exceed this time result in an estimate of aerobic capacity below the health standard; therefore, children with such scores are placed in the Needs Improvement—Health Risk Zone.

Suggestions for Test Administration

- Call out times as runners pass the start–stop line each lap to help them pace themselves.
- Test preparation should include instruction and practice in pacing. Without instruction, students usually run too fast in the early part of the test and then are forced to walk near the end. Results are generally better when students maintain a constant pace during most of the test.
- Walking is certainly permitted, but students should be encouraged to try to complete the assessment at a slow jog rather than walking. If a student cannot complete the mile distance, he or she should be assessed with the one-mile walk test (discussed next).
- Students should always warm up before taking the test and should cool down afterward by continuing to walk for several minutes after completing the distance. Students who have completed the distance can continue walking while waiting for others to finish. This approach keeps everyone moving and busy and takes the focus off of slower students, who will complete the distance last.
- The test should not be administered in unusually high temperature or humidity, or when the wind is strong, because these conditions can be unsafe and can lead to an invalid estimate of aerobic capacity.
- When a relatively small course is used with younger children, it can be difficult to count laps completed and accurately record run times. Many solutions are acceptable. For example, you might pair students and have the resting partner count laps and record the time for the runner. Alternatively, older students or parents can be asked to help record results for younger students.

Walk Test

WWW VIDEO

Alternative

Another alternative to the PACER test is the one-mile walk test, which is used only with students of age 13 and older because it has not been validated with younger samples. The walk test is an excellent alternative to the PACER because it can be used for a lifetime. Secondary students should learn this assessment so that they can use it to self-assess their own fitness levels during class and after they have graduated.

Test Objective

The objective of this test is to walk one mile (1.61 kilometer) as quickly as possible while maintaining a constant pace for the entire distance. Because the assessment is based on relative heart rate for a given walking speed, the particular pace is not critical.

Equipment and Facilities

This test requires a flat, accurately measured (1-mile, or 1.61-kilometer) course, as well as stopwatches, pencils, and score sheets (see figure 6.6); in addition, heart rate monitors, if available, make the assessment much easier. The course can be measured using either a tape measure or a cross country wheel. Caution: If the track is metric or shorter than 440 yards, adjust the course as needed (1 mile = 1,609.34 meters or 1,760 yards; 400 meters = 437.45 yards). For example, on a 400-meter track, the walk should consist of four laps plus 10 yards.

Test Instructions

1. Describe the course to students and instruct them to complete the full distance at a steady, brisk walking pace that they can maintain for the entire distance.

2. It is possible to test up to 30 students at a time by dividing the group. Have each student select a partner; one is the walker, and the other is the scorer. While the walkers do the test, the scorers count laps and record the finish time.

3. As walkers cross the finish line, the elapsed time should be called out to each participant (or to his or her partner).

4. At the conclusion of the walk, each student should take a 60-second heart-rate count. The 60-second interval can be timed by a scorer or by a pace clock with a second hand that allows the walker to mark the time. If using heart rate monitors, each participant should start his or her stopwatch at the beginning of the walk and stop it at the end. The last heart rate recorded

Figure 6.6 The score sheet for the one-mile walk test is available in the accompanying web resource.

WWW REPRODUCIBLE

during the walk should be used as the walking heart rate.

Scoring

The walk test is based on the relative heart rate when walking a mile at a specific speed. Therefore, it is necessary to have an accurate measure of the mile-walk time (scored in minutes and seconds), as well as the child's BMI and 60-second heart rate. If administering the test without using the FitnessGram software to calculate aerobic capacity, you can use the FitnessGram Score Sheet calculator (spreadsheet) located at www.pyfp.org.

If using the FitnessGram software, enter the child's weight, walk time, and 60-second heart rate. The software will then estimate the child's $\dot{V}O_2$max using the Rockport Fitness Walking Test equation (Kline et al. 1987; McSwegin et al. 1998). The estimate is evaluated using the same aerobic fitness standards used for the other assessments in order to determine the feedback messages provided in the reports.

Suggestions for Test Administration

- Test preparation should include instruction and practice in pacing and in techniques for heart rate monitoring.

- Results are generally better if students maintain a constant pace during most of the test.

- Students should always warm up before taking the test and should cool down by continuing to walk for several minutes after completing the distance.

- The test should not be administered in unusually high temperature or humidity or when the wind is strong, because these elements can cause an invalid estimate of aerobic capacity as well as create an environment that may be unsafe.

KEY CONCEPTS

- Aerobic capacity is the maximum amount of oxygen that the body can use to perform work.
- Understand the association between aerobic capacity and health risks, including high blood pressure, coronary heart disease, obesity, diabetes, some forms of cancer, and other health problems in adults.
- Measurement methods for aerobic capacity include the PACER, the one-mile run, and the walk test.
- The health standards for aerobic capacity were developed on the basis of nationally representative fitness level data. Students are classified into either the Healthy Fitness Zone, the Needs Improvement Zone, or the Needs Improvement—Health Risk Zone based on the level of fitness needed for good health.
- During test administration, ensure that students have the opportunity to prepare for the test, understand the test protocols (e.g., various tones used in the PACER), and how to pace themselves.

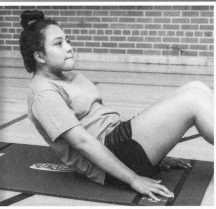

Body Composition

One's body composition is determined by the percentages of fat, bone, water, and muscle; the latter three (bone, water, and muscle) are referred to collectively as fat-free body mass. Body composition can be influenced by many factors, including age, sex, genetics, environment, and lifestyle habits related to nutrition and physical activity. Though some body fat is needed for good health, too much can lead to health problems, such as high blood pressure, high cholesterol, type 2 diabetes, and heart disease. Because youth who are overweight have a higher risk of being overweight as adults, early identification—while youth are still growing—is important. Very low levels of body fat are also unhealthy because adipose tissue stores energy and secretes a variety of essential products to regulate energy balance and other tissues. For all of these reasons, information about body composition constitutes important health information, whether one's body composition values fall into the desired Healthy Fitness Zone or one of the Needs Improvement Zones indicative of potential risks.

A number of methods are available for estimating body fatness; the most commonly used field methods are skinfold measurement and bioelectrical impedance analysis (BIA). The skinfold approach involves measuring skinfold thickness at various parts of the body using a calibrated tool referred to as a caliper. The FitnessGram skinfold procedure uses two sites that are easy to measure and whose measurements are not very invasive: triceps and calf. Measurements from these sites are used in prediction equations to estimate body fatness.

Bioelectrical impedance analysis uses a very different approach by sending a small current through the body and measuring the body's resistance to the flow of the current. A body with more muscle has lower resistance than does a body with more fat. Although this method was originally used only in research, a number of portable BIA devices are now commercially available at prices that are reasonable for most physical education programs. These devices can estimate body composition faster than a skinfold test can, and they do not require specific skill or experience to operate. In addition, the procedure is less invasive than skinfold testing and therefore may be more accepted in districts that have specific policies against the use of skinfold calipers. However, the intuitive nature of skinfold testing (pinching the skin and fat to be measured with the caliper) also provides unique educational advantages by having students actually see their skinfold pinch and the size of it. Regardless of which approach is used, the estimates can have as much as a 2 to 3 percent measurement error.

Because BIA devices are not always available, and the skinfold test is somewhat invasive and complicated to perform properly, body composition is often evaluated using a simple anthropometric measure known as body mass index (BMI). BMI is easily calculated (weight in kilograms divided by the square of height in meters) and is highly correlated with body fatness and metabolic risk factors. The BMI assessment provides useful information for most children; however, as with any screening test, there is potential for misclassification. For example, the usefulness of BMI is limited by the fact that it does not account for an individual's proportion of muscle mass. As a result, some children with high levels of muscle mass (i.e., with an athletic build) may receive a score indicating that they are too heavy for their height (i.e., that they fall into one of the Needs Improvement zones) when in fact their body composition is healthy.

Similarly, a student might have a high level of fat yet still fall into the Healthy Fitness Zone, though this error is less likely. In addition, in young children, the difference of a few inches or pounds can cause an individual of seemingly normal weight to be misclassified as overweight (i.e., it can render a false positive). With these various possibilities in mind, teachers and school administrators must be able to interpret scores in a savvy manner and answer questions about BMI from both children and parents. If questions arise, it may be appropriate to perform a follow-up assessment or provide a referral to a physician.

Overall, if properly administered and used, body composition assessment provides valuable information about a child's current weight status, as well as opportunities for education about energy balance and weight control. One advantage of using BMI for this assessment is that it allows for more direct comparison with public health data released from state and national health departments. This chapter provides details about how to administer and score these various assessments of body composition.

Additional Resources

Additional information about body composition assessment can be found in the *FitnessGram/ActivityGram Reference Guide* (Plowman and Meredith 2013), which can be downloaded at www.cooperinstitute.org/reference-guide.

OVERVIEW OF FITNESSGRAM STANDARDS FOR BODY COMPOSITION

The use of criterion-referenced standards is a unique and defining characteristic of the FitnessGram program. The standards for body fatness were developed by members of the FitnessGram Scientific Advisory Board based on data from the National Health and Nutrition Examination Surveys from 1999 through 2004 (NHANES). The NHANES data set is unique in that it is based on a representative sample of children and youth from across the country. The FitnessGram body-fat standards take into account growth and maturation and reflect a child's current risk for metabolic syndrome—a significant health problem viewed as a precursor to diabetes. Detailed information about the development of the standards is provided in the *FitnessGram/ActivityGram Reference Guide* (Plowman and Meredith 2013) and in a comprehensive research supplement published in the *American Journal of Preventive Medicine* (Morrow, Going, and Welk 2011).

A parallel set of FitnessGram BMI standards was developed to correspond with the standards established for body fatness, but these standards differed from the growth charts provided by the U.S. Centers for Disease Control and Prevention (CDC), which are commonly used by physicians. Although the differences between the CDC values and the FitnessGram standards were small in absolute terms, they caused some children to be classified differently by the two methods. Therefore, The Cooper Institute commissioned an additional set of analyses to compare the predictive utility of the FitnessGram standards with that of the CDC values. The study used additional rounds of NHANES data and evaluated the classification differences between the alternative schemes. The analyses revealed that there were no statistically significant differences between the approaches and that both had similar clinical utility. Therefore, the CDC standards have been adopted as the BMI standards in FitnessGram so that youth can receive consistent information from FitnessGram and the widely used CDC growth charts.

The FitnessGram body-fat standards allow classification in three zones that can be operationalized similarly to the commonly used categories of normal weight, overweight, and obese. Students are placed in the Healthy Fitness Zone if they have a healthy level of body fatness *or* a normal weight classification according to the CDC BMI values. They are placed in the Needs Improvement Zone if they are in the overweight category and in the Needs Improvement—Health Risk Zone if they are in the obese category. Because there are also risks associated with being too lean, FitnessGram classification options for body composition also include a fourth category—the Very Lean Zone. Youth who score in this category receive feedback about the importance of healthy eating and activity. Although some children are naturally very lean, parents must be made aware if their child's body composition places

him or her in this category. Figure 7.1 provides an overview of body composition standards for males and females.

Percent body fat and BMI provide different perspectives on a child's body composition. The two assessments are based on different measures and cannot be expected to provide consistent information for all youth or to provide similar group distributions. However, the FitnessGram standards have been set up so that the BMI standards can be interpreted in a similar manner as the standards for percent body fat. Therefore, students receive similar information regardless of whether they are placed in a given category on the basis of assessment with percent body fat or assessment with BMI.

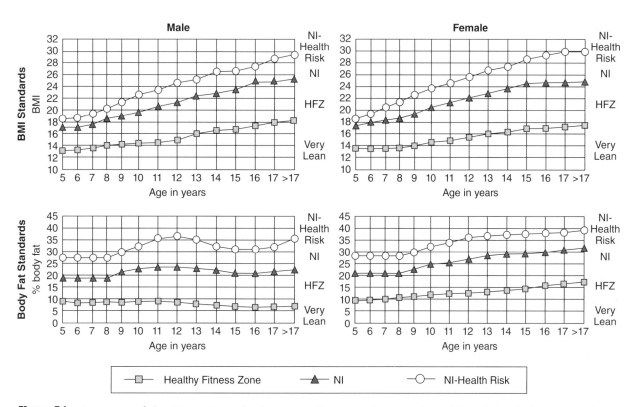

Figure 7.1 Overview of the FitnessGram body composition standards: male and female body-fat standards.

Body Mass Index

Body mass index provides an indication of the appropriateness of a child's weight relative to height. BMI is determined by the following formula: BMI = weight (kilograms) / height^2 (meters). Here is an example to demonstrate how weight and height interact to influence the BMI score. A student who weighs 100 pounds (45.36 kilograms) and is 5 feet (1.52 meters) tall has a BMI of 19.6; however, another student who weighs the same but is 5 feet 2 inches (1.57 meters) tall has a BMI of 18.3. In other words, in this case, the same weight is more appropriate for the slightly taller person, and that person's BMI is slightly lower. The following subsections describe how to accurately collect height and weight data and how to interpret the results.

Equipment

To collect accurate information about BMI, one must obtain accurate measures of height and weight. To obtain accurate height measures, we recommend using a stadiometer; the use of a tape measure attached to a wall does not provide data with the same level of accuracy. For weight, we recommend using a high-quality digital scale. Portable stadiometers and digital scales can be purchased for reasonable prices and constitute a worthwhile investment.

Test Instructions

1. To obtain accurate data about height and weight, measure children with their shoes off; shoes can be heavy and can significantly increase a person's height.

2. In measuring height and weight, enter fractions (of an inch or pound) of up to two decimal places as needed. Do not round height and weight measurements—fractions of an inch or a pound can make a difference in the calculated BMI.

Scoring

The general threshold defining overweight in adults is a BMI value greater than 25 for both males and females. Among youth, however, boys and girls have very different BMI values due to the dramatic changes in growth and development that occur with age. Therefore, age- and sex-specific values of BMI are used to assess weight status for youth. Recommended BMI scores are listed in chapter 10.

A score that falls into the Needs Improvement Zone generally indicates that a child weighs too much for his or her height. However, body mass index merely provides information about the appropriateness of the weight relative to the height. For children found to be too heavy for their height, a test of percent body fat can clarify whether the weight is due to excess fat.

Teachers who use the FitnessGram software should enter the height and weight values into the software, which will automatically calculate a BMI score. Teachers who do not have access to the FitnessGram software can use the FitnessGram Score Sheet calculator (spreadsheet), which is available at www.pyfp.org.

Bioelectrical Impedance Analysis

A number of portable BIA devices are now commercially available for less than $100. These devices estimate body composition by measuring the body's resistance to the flow of current. A body with more muscle also has more total water and therefore lower resistance to current flow. In contrast, a body with more fat has less total water and therefore greater resistance to current flow.

BIA devices can produce estimates of body composition faster than a skinfold test can, and they do not require specific skill or experience. The procedure is also less invasive than skinfold testing and therefore may be more accepted in districts that have specific policies against the use of skinfold calipers. Measurement results with these devices are comparable to skinfold measurement in terms of classification accuracy and body composition estimates.

Test Instructions

Follow the instructions accompanying the device that you are using for the test. One type of BIA device requires participants to stand on an instrument resembling a bathroom scale while barefoot. Another type has participants squeeze handles while extending their arms.

Scoring

The output from the BIA device is the measure of percent body fat. You can use this result and the Healthy Fitness Zone standards chart presented in chapter 10 to determine how to classify each student's level of body fatness.

Skinfold Measurements

Skinfolds are reliable (give similar results with repeated measures) measures of body composition, providing the tester has sufficient training and experience in the skinfold measurement approach and has followed the standardized protocols for triceps and medial calf skinfold measurements. This section includes suggestions for learning how to do skinfold measurements.

Skinfold measurement requires the teacher to touch each student on the back of the arm and the inside of the leg. Some school districts and schools may have policies about this type of testing. Teachers who want to do the skinfold test should check local policies prior to beginning the testing. In many schools, the nurse is asked to administer the skinfold assessment.

If the school district or school does not allow skinfold measurement, the teacher is encouraged to use the BIA device technique to assess body composition.

Equipment

This measurement requires a skinfold caliper, which is designed to measure the thickness of a double layer of subcutaneous fat and skin at different parts of the body. The cost of a skinfold caliper ranges from $5 to $200; the quality off the caliper is less important than training and practice in using it for body composition assessment.

Test Instructions

Multiple procedures exist for skinfold testing; the FitnessGram protocol involves collecting measures from the triceps and calf. These sites have been chosen for FitnessGram because they are easily measured and highly correlated with total body fatness. An additional measure from the abdominal site is used for college students because by college-age students have begun to deposit adipose tissue on the trunk. The following subsections provide details about these measurement sites, as well as specific measurement tips.

- **Triceps.** The triceps skinfold is measured on the back of the right arm over the triceps muscle, midway between the elbow and the acromion process of the scapula (figure 7.2a). A ruler, measuring tape, or piece of string can be used to find the midpoint. The skinfold site should be vertical. Pinch the fold slightly above the midpoint to ensure that the fold is measured right on the midpoint (figures 7.2, b and c).

- **Calf.** The calf skinfold is measured on the inside of the right leg at the level of maximal calf girth. The right foot is placed flat on an elevated surface with the knee flexed at a 90 degree angle (figure 7.3a). The vertical skinfold should be grasped just above the level of maximal girth (figure 7.3b), and the measurement should be made below the grasp.

- **Abdominal area (college students only).** The FitnessGram assessment can be used through age 25. For college students, the formula for calculating percent body fat includes the abdominal skinfold measurement in addition to the triceps and calf skinfolds. The abdominal skinfold is measured at a site located 3 centimeters to the side of the midpoint of the umbilicus and 1 centimeter below it (figure 7.4a). The skinfold is horizontal and should be measured on the right side of the body (figure 7.4b) while the subject relaxes the abdominal wall as much as possible.

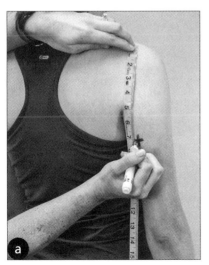
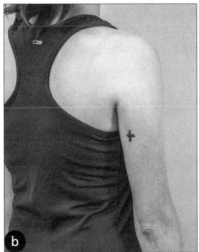
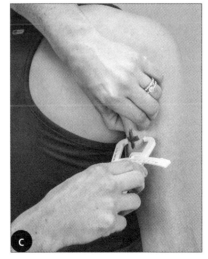

Figure 7.2 *(a)* Locating the triceps skinfold site. *(b)* Site of the triceps skinfold. *(c)* Triceps skinfold measurement.

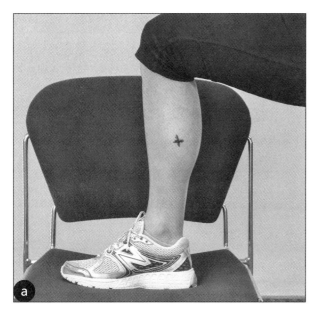
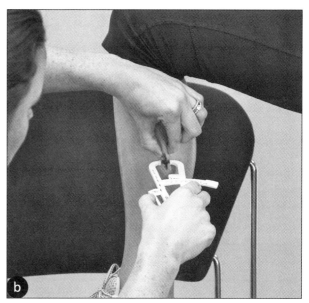

Figure 7.3 *(a)* Placement of the leg for locating the calf skinfold site. *(b)* Calf skinfold measurement.

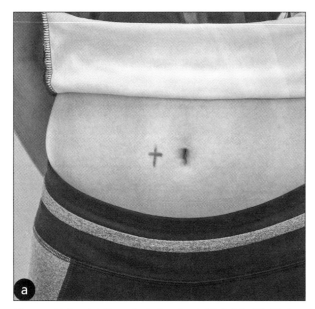
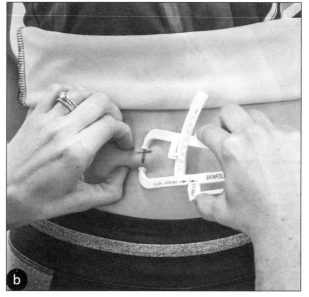

Figure 7.4 *(a)* Site of abdominal skinfold. *(b)* Abdominal skinfold measurement.

To obtain accurate information from skinfold measurements, use standardized techniques and conduct assessments as consistently as possible. Here are some tips for making accurate skinfold measurements:

- Standard skinfold measurement protocol indicates that these measurements should be taken on the right side of the body unless there is a specific reason that they cannot be taken there (for example, scar tissue at the measurement site). If a measurement cannot be made on the right side, then both measures should be done on the left side of the body.

- Instruct the student to relax the arm or leg being measured.
- Firmly grasp the skinfold between the thumb and forefinger and lift it away from the other body tissue. The grasp should not be so firm as to be painful.
- Place the caliper 0.5 inch (1.27 centimeters) below the pinch site.
- Be sure that the caliper is in the middle of the fold.
- Take one measurement at each site before doing the second measurement at each site and finally the third set of measurements at each site.

Scoring

The skinfold procedure requires accurate estimates of skinfold thicknesses (measured in millimeters) as shown on the caliper. Each measurement should be taken three times, and the recorded score should be the median (middle) value of the three scores. To illustrate: If the readings are 7.0, 9.0, and 8.0, the recorded score is 8.0 millimeters. Each reading should be recorded to the nearest 0.5 millimeter. For teachers not using the FitnessGram software, the accompanying web resource includes percent-fatness look-up charts for boys and for girls (see figure 7.5, *a* and *b*). FitnessGram uses the formula developed by Slaughter and Lohman to calculate percent body fat (Slaughter et al. 1988).

Suggestions for Test Administration

- Body composition testing should be conducted in a setting that provides the child with privacy.
- Interpretation of the measurements may be given in a group setting as long as individual results are not identified and students are not allowed to compare scores.
- Whenever possible, have the same tester conduct all measurements for all students in a class to maximize consistency.
- Practice, practice, practice. Practice taking measurements on many students and other people before actually trying to do the measuring for the fitness assessment. You should also practice by measuring the same individual multiple times to test your accuracy. As you become familiar with

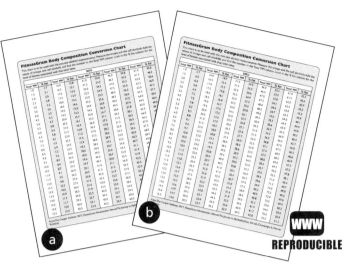

Figure 7.5 Body-composition conversion charts are available in the accompanying web resource for *(a)* boys and *(b)* girls.

the methods, you can generally achieve agreement within a margin of 10 percent between testers.

Learning to Do Skinfold Measurements

Obtaining consistently accurate skinfold measurements requires training and experience. Video training and workshop participation are two excellent ways for educators to learn how to do skinfold measurements or to refresh their skills. The accompanying web resource contains protocol videos to help you learn the procedures described in this manual.

KEY CONCEPTS

- Body composition is determined by the proportions of fat mass and fat-free mass in the body.
- Assessment methods for determining percent body fat include bioelectrical impedance analysis and skinfold measurement.
- Body mass index is an alternative measure that uses height and weight to provide information about the appropriateness of an individual's weight in relation to his or her height.
- Understand the relationship between excess body fat and risk factors for coronary heart disease, stroke, and diabetes among children.
- FitnessGram BMI standards align with CDC growth charts, which are commonly used by physicians.
- During test administration, provide privacy for students and practice taking measurements to maximize accuracy and consistency.

Muscular Strength, Endurance, and Flexibility

In FitnessGram, tests of muscular strength, muscular endurance, and flexibility are combined into one broad fitness category because the primary purpose is to determine the functional health of the musculoskeletal system. Muscular strength is the *maximal* force that your muscles can exert in a *single* effort. Muscular endurance, on the other hand, is the ability to *sustain* or *repeat* muscular activity over time. Flexibility is the range of motion at a joint. It is equally important to have strong muscles that can work forcefully and over a period of time and to be flexible enough to have a full range of motion at the relevant joint. Muscle imbalance at a specific joint can result in musculoskeletal injury; specifically, the muscles on one side may be much stronger than the opposing muscles or may be insufficiently flexible to allow complete motion or sudden motion.

The development of musculoskeletal strength, endurance, and flexibility is directly affected by the specificity of training. Although the FitnessGram assessment items are only a sampling of the ways a body moves, they do measure muscle strength, muscle endurance, and also flexibility in the upper body, trunk, and lower body.

We recommend assessing musculoskeletal fitness by conducting tests of the upper body and the abdominal and trunk areas because of their relationship to activities of daily living, good posture, and back health. FitnessGram test items and methods are carefully selected to be safe, reliable, and valid. A balanced, healthy, well-functioning musculoskeletal system can exert force, resist fatigue, and move freely through a full range of motion. This musculoskeletal fitness helps an individual perform daily activities more easily, reduces the risk of injury, and improves abdominal and back health. Most important, when we help children and youth understand the status of their muscular strength, endurance, and flexibility, they can carry this understanding forward into adulthood, thus preventing many health problems and improving their quality of life.

Goals for a healthy back include proper alignment of the vertebrae and pelvis, freedom from excessive disc pressure, and pelvic ability to rotate forward and backward without strain on the muscles or connective tissue. To accomplish these goals an individual must have sufficient—but not excessive—flexibility of the low-back, hamstring, and hip-flexor muscles, as well as strong, fatigue-resistant abdominal and trunk extensor muscles. Although most students can achieve the criterion-referenced standards for one or two test items, they still need to be educated about the importance of muscular strength, muscular endurance, and flexibility for preventing problems in adulthood. It is especially important to make students aware of correct postural alignment and body mechanics in the event that they are developing scoliosis, which is a problem associated with teenagers. Good sources of information about scoliosis include school nurses, local physicians, and physical therapists.

Throughout this chapter, you have the option of scoring students' performances and recording their scores yourself or allowing students to assist each other in scoring and recording scores. If students record scores, each student should be given a copy of the Personal Fitness Record (figure 5.1, *a* or *b*), which is available in the web resource. If you record scores, use the Class Score Sheet (figure 5.1*c*) from the web resource or from the FitnessGram software.

To help students determine whether their scores place them in the Healthy Fitness Zone, refer to the Healthy Fitness Zone standards charts (figure 5.2, *a* and *b*), which are available in the web resource.

Additional Resources

More information about the reliability and validity of musculoskeletal fitness testing is provided in the *FitnessGram/Activity-Gram Reference Guide* (Plowman and Meredith 2013), which can be downloaded at www.cooperinstitute.org/reference-guide. The guide also includes information about the derivation of the FitnessGram Healthy Fitness Zone criteria.

ABDOMINAL STRENGTH AND ENDURANCE

Strength and endurance of the abdominal muscles are important in promoting good posture and correct pelvic alignment, the latter of which is particularly important to low-back health. In testing and training the muscles of this region, it is difficult to isolate specific abdominal muscles. For example, the modified sit-up, which is used in many fitness tests, involves the hip flexor muscles in addition to the abdominal muscles. In contrast, the curl-up assessment used in FitnessGram is both safer and more effective because it does not involve the hip flexor muscles and because it minimizes compression in the spine, as compared with a full sit-up in which the feet are held. This protocol is adapted from a version reported by Massicote (1990).

Curl-Up

Recommended

WWW
VIDEO

The curl-up with knees flexed and feet unanchored is used because these two elements have been shown to do the following: (a) decrease movement of the fifth lumbar vertebra over the sacral vertebrae, (b) minimize activation of the hip flexors, (c) increase the activation of the external and internal obliques and transverse abdominals, and (d) maximize abdominal muscle activation of the lower and upper rectus abdominals relative to disc compression (load) as compared with a variety of sit-ups. Specific research studies related to the curl-up are discussed in the *FitnessGram/ActivityGram Reference Guide* (Plowman and Meredith 2013), which can be downloaded at www.cooperinstitute.org/reference-guide. The consistency and accuracy of the curl-up assessment have been addressed by only a few results. Reliability is higher for college students than for children, but the values for children are acceptable for this type of assessment. Determination of validity has been hampered by the lack of an established criterion measure. The primary support for using the curl-up test to determine abdominal strength and endurance has been provided through anatomical analysis and electromyographical documentation.

Test Objective

The objective of this test is to complete as many curl-ups as possible (up to a maximum of 75) at a specified pace.

Equipment and Facilities

This test requires a gym mat marked with the distances of the curl-up strips or a gym mat and a measuring strip for every two students. Premarked mats are available for purchase, or you can make curl-up strips from cardboard, rubber, smooth wood, or any similar material that is thin and flat and measures 30 to 35 inches (76.2 to 88.9 centimeters) in length. Two widths of measuring strip may be needed—a narrower width (3 inches, or 7.62 centimeters) for testing 5- to 9-year-olds and a wider one (4.5 inches, or 11.43 centimeters) for testing older students. You also need score sheets, either for individuals (figure 5.1, *a* or *b*) or for the class (figure 5.1c); these sheets are available in the web resource.

During the test, you will need the curl-up test cadence from the accompanying web resource and a device with which to play the cadence (e.g., laptop or other digital music player with speaker).

WWW
CADENCE

Test Instructions

1. Allow students to partner up in groups of two. Partner A will perform the curl-up while partner B counts and watches for form errors.

2. Partner A lies supine on the mat with knees bent at an angle of about 140 degrees, feet flat on the floor, legs slightly apart, arms straight and parallel to the trunk, and palms resting on the mat. The fingers are stretched out, and the head is in contact with the mat. Make sure that students extend their feet as far as possible from the buttocks while still allowing the feet to remain flat on the floor—the closer the feet are to the buttocks, the more difficult the movement.

3. After partner A assumes position on the mat, partner B ensures that the fingertips rest on the nearest edge of the curl-up distance by checking the location on a premarked mat or by placing the measuring strip on the mat under partner A's legs so that partner A's fingertips are on the nearest edge of the measuring strip (figure 8.1a).

4. Partner B then kneels down at partner A's head in a position to count curl-ups and watch for form

breaks. Partner B places a piece of paper under partner A's head to help determine whether partner A's head touches down on each repetition (the paper crinkles each time partner A touches it with his or her head).

5. Before the test begins, partner B may pull on partner A's hands to ensure that the shoulders are relaxed and in a normal resting position. If partner A is allowed to hunch the shoulders before beginning the test, he or she may be able to get the fingertips to the other side of the testing strip by merely moving the arms and shoulders up and down.

6. The test begins with the feet flat on the floor but only the heels must remain in contact with the mat during the test. Partner A curls up slowly (figure 8.1b), sliding the fingers across the measuring strip until they reach the other side (figure 8.2, a and b). Partner A then curls back down until his or her head touches the piece of paper on the mat. Movement should be slow and gauged to the cadence of about 20 curl-ups per minute (1 every three seconds); the teacher either calls the cadence or uses the prerecorded cadence. The performer should not be allowed to reach forcibly with the arms and hands.

7. Partner A continues without pausing until he or she can no longer continue or has completed 75 curl-ups, or until the second form correction is made.

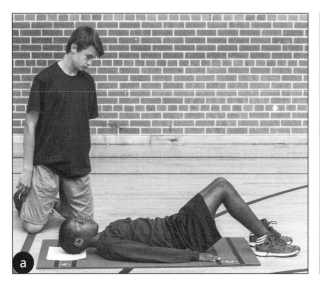 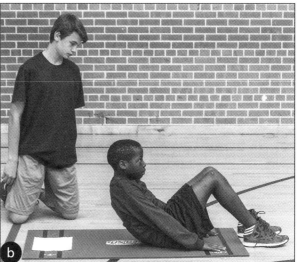

Figure 8.1 *(a)* Starting position for the curl-up test. *(b)* "Up" position in the curl-up test.

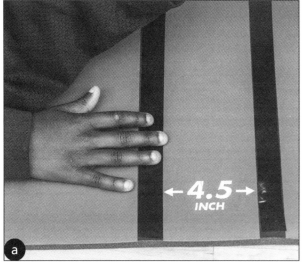 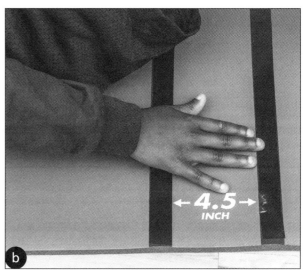

Figure 8.2 *(a)* Close-up of fingertips sliding in the starting position. *(b)* Close-up of fingertips sliding in the ending position.

Form Corrections

- The heels must remain in contact with the floor.
- The head must return to the mat on each repetition.
- Pauses and rest periods are not allowed; the movement should be continuous and in keeping with the cadence.
- The fingertips must touch the far side of the measuring strip.

Scoring

The score is the number of curl-ups performed. A curl-up should be counted when the student's head returns to the mat. For ease in administration, the first form break counts as a curl-up; the test ends on the second form break.

Suggestions for Test Administration

- The student being tested should reposition if the body moves so that the head does not contact the mat at the appropriate spot or if the measuring strip is out of position.

- Movement should start with a flattening of the lower back, followed by a slow curling of the upper spine.
- The hands should slide across the measuring strip until the fingertips reach the opposite side (either 3 or 4.5 inches), then return to the supine position. The movement is complete when the back of the head touches the paper placed on the mat.
- The cadence encourages steady, continuous movement done with correct form.
- Students should not reach forcibly with their arms and hands; nonetheless, when students first begin to perform this test item, they may want to reach, especially if they have previously done a timed sit-up test. In this test, however, they should simply let their arms move passively along the floor in response to the action of the trunk and shoulders. Any jerking, kipping, or reaching motion causes the student to move out of position.
- This curl-up protocol is quite different from that of the one-minute sit-up. Students need to learn how to correctly perform the curl-up movement and must be allowed time to practice it.

TRUNK EXTENSOR STRENGTH AND FLEXIBILITY

A test of trunk extensor strength and flexibility is included in FitnessGram because of its relationship to low-back health, especially proper vertebral alignment. Good levels of musculoskeletal fitness in the abdominal muscles, hamstrings, and back extensors work in concert to maintain good posture and low-back health. This test item is included in the assessment in part because of the educational value of simply doing it, which helps students learn that trunk extensor strength and flexibility are important aspects of maintaining a healthy back.

Trunk Lift

Recommended

This test requires close attention to performance technique. The movement should be performed in a slow and controlled manner. The maximum score on the test is 12 inches (30.48 centimeters); although some flexibility is important, hyperextension is neither advisable nor safe.

Specific research references regarding the trunk lift may be found in the *FitnessGram/ActivityGram Reference Guide* (Plowman and Meredith 2013), which can be downloaded at www.cooperinstitute.org/reference-guide. Test–retest studies of the trunk extension test (done without limiting the lift to 12 inches) have reported high reliability in high school and college-age students. No data have been established regarding the consistency of results for younger children.

Research results have shown that performance of the trunk lift involves contributions from isokinetic trunk endurance, torso length, body weight, passive trunk extension, trunk extension endurance, trunk strength, and flexibility. However, given that this test is a single-repetition, restricted-range item partially limited by body weight, it provides only a minimal assessment of the components of trunk strength and flexibility. Therefore, it will be passed easily by most school-age individuals. The test experience does serve to focus attention on this aspect of fitness and to inform students that trunk strength, endurance, and flexibility are important for good health.

Test Objective

The objective of this test is to lift the upper body off of the floor by using the muscles of the back and then to hold the position to allow for the measurement.

Equipment and Facilities

This test requires gym mats and a measuring device—preferably a yardstick (or meter stick) or 15-inch (38.1-centimeter) ruler, though a 12-inch (30.48-centimeter) ruler can be used if care is taken not to place it directly under the student's chin, which would pose a serious safety hazard because the raised position can be difficult to maintain for some students. For the same reason, if students measure each other's lifts, they should use rulers made of a pliable material (e.g., poster board) and marked with tape at 6 inches (15.24 centimeters), 9 inches (22.86 centimeters), and 12 inches (30.48 centimeters); another option is to use a 12-inch rope marked with tape in a similar manner. As described in the test instructions, a coin or other marker (e.g., poker chip) is also needed for spotting. Use either individual score sheets (figure 5.1, *a* or *b*) or class score sheets (figure 5.1*c*), all of which are available in the web resource.

Test Instructions

1. The student being tested lies prone (facedown) on the mat with the toes pointed and the hands under the thighs and with the chin in a neutral position causing the face to be looking directly at the mat.

2. Place a coin or other marker on the floor in line with the student's eyes. During the movement, the student's face should not look forward; that is, the student's focus should not move from the coin or marker.

3. The student lifts the upper body off of the floor in a very slow and controlled manner to a maximum height of 12 inches (figure 8.3, *a* and *b*). The head should be maintained in a neutral (straight) alignment with the spine.

4. The raised position is held long enough to allow the tester to place the ruler on the floor *in front of or to the side of* the student's chin and determine the distance from the floor to the student's chin. More specifically, the ruler should be placed at least 1 inch (2.54 centimeters) in front of or to the side of the student's chin—*not* directly under the chin.

5. Once the measurement has been made, the student returns to the starting position in a controlled manner.

6. Conduct two trials and record the highest score.

Figure 8.3 *(a)* Starting position for the trunk lift. *(b)* Measurement of the trunk lift.

Scoring

The score is recorded in inches or centimeters; distances beyond 12 inches (30.48 centimeters) should be recorded as 12 inches.

Suggestions for Test Administration

- Do not allow students to do ballistic, bouncing movements.
- Do not encourage students to lift the chin more than 12 inches (30.48 centimeters). The Healthy Fitness Zone ends at 12 inches, and scores beyond 12 inches are recorded as 12 inches. Excessive arching of the back can cause compression of the spinal discs.
- Maintaining focus on the marker on the floor helps the performer keep the head in a neutral position.
- Partner B makes the reading at eye level and therefore assumes a squatting or lying position.

UPPER-BODY STRENGTH AND ENDURANCE

Strength and endurance in the upper-body muscles are important in activities of daily living and in maintaining functional health and promoting good posture. The role of upper-body strength in maintaining functionality becomes more evident as a person ages; therefore, it is important that children and youth learn the importance of upper-body strength and endurance, as well as methods for developing and maintaining this area of fitness. The recommended test item in this area is the 90 degree push-up, which is adapted from assessments reported by Massicote (1990); alternative options include the modified pull-up and the flexed arm hang. Although all of these items are intended to measure upper-arm and shoulder-girdle strength and endurance, they do not all involve the same muscle groups to the same extent; in addition, handling body weight is more of a factor in some items than in others.

90 Degree Push-Up

Recommended

The 90 degree push-up (to an elbow angle of 90 degrees) is the recommended test for upper-body strength and endurance. It offers multiple advantages: administration of the test requires little or no equipment, multiple students can be tested at once, and few zero scores are produced. In addition, the test teaches students an activity that they can use throughout life not only for self-testing but also as a conditioning activity.

Specific research references regarding the push-up may be found in the *FitnessGram/ActivityGram Reference Guide* (Plowman and Meredith 2013), which can be downloaded at www.cooperinstitute.org/reference-guide. The push-up test has been shown to produce generally consistent scores, but reliability depends on how it is administered. Objectivity, or the ability of different observers to produce the same results, is a factor in this item because of the necessity of judging the 90 degree angle. Lower values have been reported for elementary-age students who use partners to count repetitions. Specifically, scores from student partners are consistently higher than adult counts because students tend to simply count each attempted 90 degree push-up without evaluating whether it was done correctly.

As with several of the other neuromuscular fitness items, it is difficult to determine the accuracy of the 90 degree push-up as a test (in this case of upper-body strength and endurance) due to the lack of an agreed-upon criterion measure. Specific validation data are available for the 90 degree push-up in only two studies, which were conducted on college-age students. In these studies, validity coefficients against a 1-repetition max (1RM) bench press were highest when the criterion test was the number of repetitions (endurance) at an absolute, but sex-specific, load.

This test can be challenging for students because they must first understand what the 90 degree angle looks like and then what it feels like. Before test day, students should be allowed to practice doing 90 degree push-ups and watching a partner do them. Make a concerted effort during these practice sessions to correct students who are not achieving the 90 degree angle. To help students visualize the angle, have them explore making it with different body parts; specifically, see if they can make it with their arms, legs, hands, and body (figure 8.4, *a* and *b*).

Once students are familiar with the 90 degree angle, have them practice what it feels like when doing a push-up. With students working in pairs, assign one partner to perform the push-up and the other to serve as the "90 degree guide." Have the guide place a flat hand in the crease of the performing student's elbow while the performer is in the "up" (raised) position of the movement. When the student performing the push-up is ready, he or she lowers the body by bending the arms until the elbows are at a 90 degree angle. When the upper arm touches the guide's palm or back of hand (depending on whether the palm is facing up or down), the upper arms should be parallel to the floor and the elbows bent at 90 degrees. This touch indicates to the performer that he or she has achieved the 90 degree angle; the guide can also provide verbal feedback. Have the performer complete several repetitions, then have the partners switch roles. Remember, it is important for students to practice before conducting the official test.

Test Objective

To complete as many 90 degree push-ups as possible at a rhythmic pace (up to a maximum of 75).

Figure 8.4 *(a)* Starting position for the 90 degree push-up test. *(b)* Student in the "down" (lowered) position for the 90 degree push-up test.

Equipment and Facilities

The 90 degree push-up can be performed on a mat, and a cardboard square or other object with a 90 degree angle can be used to help students judge the angle. Use score sheets either for individuals (figure 5.1, *a* or *b*) or for the class (figure 5.1*c*), all of which are available in the web resource.

You will need the 90 degree push-up test cadence from the accompanying web resource and a device with which to play the cadence (e.g., laptop or other digital music player with speaker). The correct cadence calls for 20 push-ups per minute (i.e., 1 every three seconds).

Test Instructions

1. Students should be paired; one performs the test while the other counts 90 degree push-ups and watches to see that the performer bends the elbows to 90 degrees with the upper arms parallel to the floor.

2. The performer assumes a prone position on the mat with the hands under or slightly wider than the shoulders, the fingers stretched out, the legs straight and slightly apart, and the toes tucked under.

3. The performer pushes up off of the mat with the arms until the arms are straight, keeping the legs and back straight. The back should be kept in a straight line from head to toes throughout the test (figure 8.4*a*).

4. The performer then lowers the body with the arms until the elbows bend at a 90 degree angle and the upper arms are parallel to the floor (figure 8.4*b*).

5. This movement is repeated as many times as possible. On each repetition, the performer should push up until the arms are straight.

6. The rhythm should be approximately 20 push-ups per minute (1 every three seconds).

7. The performer is stopped upon making the second form correction (mistake).

Form Corrections

- Stopping to rest or not maintaining a rhythmic pace
- Not achieving a 90 degree angle with the elbow
- Not maintaining correct body position with a straight back
- Not extending the arms fully

Scoring

The score is the number of 90 degree push-ups performed. For ease in administration, the first form break is counted as a push-up; the test ends on the second form break.

Suggestions for Test Administration

- The test should be terminated if the student appears to be in extreme discomfort or pain.
- The cadence should be called or played from the accompanying web resource.
- Males and females follow the same protocol.
- Use a piece of pliable equipment, such as a short cone or large foam ball, that can be placed under the student's chest. The student must lower to the equipment in order for the 90 degree push-up to count. The appropriate height of the equipment depends on the size of your students.

Modified Pull-Up

Alternative

Like the 90 degree push-up, the modified pull-up offers the advantage of few zero scores and a wide range of scores. However, it does not, as commonly believed, negate the effect of body composition and weight on upper-body performance. Still, it is a very good test item for educators who have access to appropriate equipment and want to test students individually.

Specific research references regarding the modified pull-up may be found in the *FitnessGram/ActivityGram Reference Guide* (Plowman and Meredith 2013), which can be downloaded at www.cooperinstitute.org/reference-guide. The modified pull-up has been found to be a reliable test in primary, middle, and high school students. It has not been validated against a criterion measure but does have logical validity based on anatomical principles.

Test Objective

The objective of this test is to complete as many modified pull-ups as possible (up to a maximum of 150).

Equipment and Facilities

This test requires a modified pull-up stand, a pencil, and score sheets either for individuals (figure 5.1, *a* or *b*) or for the class (figure 5.1*c*); these score sheets are available in the web resource. The assessment should be performed on a mat or other soft surface.

Test Instructions

1. Position the student on his or her back with the shoulders directly under a bar set 1 to 2 inches (2.54 to 5.08 centimeters) above the student's reach.
2. The bar should have a measuring device hanging down 7 to 8 inches (17.78 to 20.32 centimeters) below the bar.

3. The student grasps the bar with an overhand grip (palms away from body). The pull-up begins in this "down" position with the arms and legs straight, the buttocks off of the floor, and only the heels touching the floor (figure 8.5*a*).
4. The student pulls up until the chest touches the measuring device (figure 8.5*b*).
5. The student lowers the body to the "down" position. Movement continues in a rhythmic manner.
6. The student is stopped when the second form correction is made. There is no time limit, but movement should be rhythmic and continuous; the student should not stop to rest.

Form Corrections

- Stopping to rest or not maintaining a rhythmic pace
- Not lifting the chest to the measuring device
- Not maintaining a straight body position with only the heels in contact with the floor
- Not fully extending the arms in the down position

Scoring

The score is the number of modified pull-ups performed. For ease in administration, the first form break is counted as a pull-up. The test ends on the second form break.

Suggestions for Test Administration

- The test is terminated if the student experiences extreme discomfort or pain.
- Males and females follow the same protocol.

Figure 8.5 *(a)* Starting position for the modified pull-up test. *(b)* Student in the "up" position for the modified pull-up test.

Flexed Arm Hang

Alternative

The second alternative to the recommended 90 degree push-up is the flexed arm hang. This option is a static test of upper-body strength and endurance. Specific research references regarding the flexed arm hang may be found in the *FitnessGram/ActivityGram Reference Guide* (Plowman and Meredith 2013), which can be downloaded at www.cooperinstitute.org/reference-guide. Consistency in performance time for the flexed arm hang has been found acceptable in both 9- and 10-year-olds and in college-age students. In terms of validity, two studies have attempted to validate the flexed arm hang against the 1RM arm curl for endurance but found only weak correlations. Therefore, as with most of the other upper-body tests, only anatomical logic validates this item.

Test Objective

The objective of this test is to hang with the chin above the bar for as long as possible (up to a maximum of 999 seconds).

Equipment and Facilities

This test requires a horizontal bar, a chair or stool (optional), a stopwatch, and score sheets either for individuals (figure 5.1, *a* or *b*) or for the class (figure 5.1*c*); these score sheets are available in the web resource.

Test Instructions

1. The student grasps the bar with an overhand grip (palms facing away). To standardize the thumb placement for the flexed arm hang and the modified pull-up, please note that the thumb placement for both grips should encircle the bar.
2. With the assistance of one or more spotters, the student raises the body off of the floor to a position in which the chin is above the bar, the elbows are flexed, and the chest is close to the bar (figure 8.6).
3. As soon as the student takes this position, the stopwatch is started. The student holds the position as long as possible.
4. The watch is stopped when one of the following occurs:
   - The student's chin touches the bar.

Figure 8.6 Student in the "up" position for the flexed arm hang test.

   - The student tilts his or her head back to keep the chin above the bar.
   - The student's chin falls below the bar.

Scoring

The score is the number of seconds for which the student maintains the correct hanging position.

Suggestions for Test Administration

- The student's body must not swing during the test. If the student starts to swing, the teacher or assistant should hold an extended arm across the front of the thighs to prevent the swinging motion.
- Only one trial is permitted unless the teacher believes that the pupil has not had a fair opportunity to perform.

FLEXIBILITY

Maintaining adequate joint flexibility is important to functional health. For young people, however, decreased flexibility is generally not a problem, and many of your students will easily pass the flexibility item; therefore, it has been made optional in FitnessGram. If you decide not to administer the flexibility test, you should still teach students about flexibility and inform them that maintaining flexibility and range of motion will be important as they age.

Back-Saver Sit and Reach

Optional

The back-saver sit and reach is very similar to the traditional sit and reach except that the measurement is performed on one side at a time. Testing one leg at a time enables you to identify any asymmetry in hamstring flexibility; it also avoids hyperextension of the knee. The sit and reach measures predominantly the flexibility of the hamstring muscles. Normal hamstring flexibility allows rotation of the pelvis in forward bending movements and posterior tilting of the pelvis for proper sitting.

Specific research references regarding the back-saver sit and reach may be found in the *FitnessGram/ActivityGram Reference Guide* (Plowman and Meredith 2013), which can be downloaded at www.cooperinstitute.org/reference-guide. The back-saver sit and reach has been shown to provide extremely consistent scores when administered under standardized conditions. It has also been shown to be a reasonably accurate measure of hamstring flexibility; when compared with criterion measures of hamstring flexibility, the correlations for both right and left legs have been moderate to high. Conversely, the test has been shown to correlate poorly with criterion tests for low-back flexibility; therefore, it cannot be considered a valid measure of low-back flexibility and should not be interpreted as such.

Test Objective

The objective of this item is to reach the specified distance on the right and left sides of the body. The distance required to achieve the Healthy Fitness Zone is adjusted for age and sex.

Equipment and Facilities

This assessment requires a sturdy box with a height of 12 inches (30.48 centimeters). A measuring scale is placed on top of the box with the 9-inch (22.86-centimeter) mark even with the front edge of the box against which the student's foot will rest. The "zero" end of the ruler is nearest the student. Teachers may purchase devices made specifically for administering the back-saver sit and reach, or a wooden box and yardstick (or meter stick) will suffice. Tape the yardstick to the top of the box with the 9-inch mark at the nearest edge of the box and the zero end of the stick toward the student. Use score sheets either for individuals (figure 5.1, *a* or *b*) or for the class (figure 5.1*c*), all of which are available in the web resource.

Test Instructions

1. The student removes his or her shoes and sits down at the test apparatus. One leg is fully extended with the foot flat against the face of the box. The other knee is bent with the sole of the foot flat on the floor. The instep of that foot is placed in line with, and 2 to 3 inches (5.08 to 7.62 centimeters) to the side of, the straight knee. The arms are extended forward over the measuring scale with the hands placed one on top of the other (figure 8.7*a*).

2. The student reaches forward along the scale with both hands (palms down) four times, keeping the back straight and the head up, and holds the position of the fourth reach for at least one second (figure 8.7*b*). If necessary, the student may allow the bent knee to move to the side as the body moves forward, but the sole of the foot must remain on the floor.

3. After one side has been measured, the student switches the position of the legs and repeats the process. Measurement of right and left sides may be made in any order, but both sides must be measured.

Figure 8.7 *(a)* Starting position for measuring the left side. *(b)* Back-saver sit and reach stretch for the left side.

Scoring

Record the distance reached on each side to the nearest 0.5 inch (1.27 centimeter), up to a maximum score of 12 inches (30.48 centimeters); this limitation on distance is used to discourage hypermobility. To be in the Healthy Fitness Zone, the student should meet the standard on both the right and left sides.

Suggestions for Test Administration

- The bent knee can move to the side, thus allowing the body to move past it, but the sole of the same-side foot must remain on the floor.

- The back should remain straight and the head up during the forward flexion movement.

- The knee of the extended leg should remain straight. The tester may place one hand above the performer's knee to remind him or her to keep the knee straight.

- The hands should reach forward evenly.

- The trial should be repeated if the hands reach unevenly or the straight knee bends.

- The hips must remain square to the box; do not allow the student to turn the hip away from the box while reaching.

Shoulder Stretch

Optional

The shoulder stretch is a simple test of upper-arm and shoulder-girdle flexibility that is intended to parallel strength and endurance assessment of that region. If used alternately with the back-saver sit and reach, it may help students learn that flexibility is specific to each joint, that hamstring flexibility does not represent total body flexibility, and that the hamstrings are not the only area of the body where flexibility is important.

Test Objective

The objective of this test is to touch the fingertips together behind the back by reaching over the shoulder and under the elbow.

Equipment and Facilities

This test requires score sheets either for individuals (figure 5.1, a or b) or for the class (figure 5.1c), all of which are available in the web resource. No additional equipment is necessary.

Test Instructions

1. Allow students to select a partner who will judge whether the stretch is completed.
2. To test the right shoulder, partner A reaches with the right hand over the right shoulder and down the back as if to pull up a zipper or scratch between the shoulder blades. At the same time, partner A places the left hand behind the back and reaches up, trying to touch the fingers of the right hand (figure 8.8a). Partner B observes whether the fingers touch.
3. To test the left shoulder, partner A repeats the process on the other side. Specifically, he or she reaches with the left hand over the left shoulder and down the back as if to pull up a zipper or scratch between the shoulder blades. At the same time, partner A places the right hand behind the back and reaches up, trying to touch the fingers of the left hand (figure 8.8b). As with the right-side test, partner B notes whether the fingers touch.

Scoring

If the student is able to touch his or her fingers with the right hand over the shoulder, a Y (yes) is recorded for the right side; if not, an N (no) is recorded. Similarly, if the student is able to touch the fingers with the left hand over the shoulder, a Y is recorded for the left side; if not, an N is recorded. To achieve the Healthy Fitness Zone, a Y must be recorded on both the right and left sides.

Figure 8.8 (a) Shoulder stretch on the right side. (b) Shoulder stretch on the left side.

 **KEY CONCEPTS**

- FitnessGram tests that assess muscular strength, endurance, and flexibility refer to the functional health status of the musculoskeletal system.

- Muscular strength is the maximal force that your muscles can exert in a single effort.

- Muscular endurance is the ability to sustain muscular activity over time.

- Flexibility is the range of motion at a given joint.

- Recommended test items include the curl-up (for abdominal strength and endurance), the trunk lift (for trunk extensor strength and flexibility), the 90 degree push-up (for upper-body strength and endurance), and the back-saver sit and reach (for flexibility).

FitnessGram Physical Activity Questions

Physical activity questions were added to the FitnessGram assessment to improve the prescriptive information provided to the student. A child's performance on physical fitness tests can be influenced by many factors, including heredity, maturation, and body composition. Some children may get discouraged if they do not score well on fitness tests despite being active. Alternatively, children may incorrectly believe that they don't need to be active if their fitness levels are in the Healthy Fitness Zone. To help students avoid these pitfalls, the FitnessGram physical activity assessment helps them learn to associate physical activity more directly with physical fitness. If you are using the FitnessGram software, the activity assessment also allows you to provide more personalized information on the FitnessGram Report; this feedback reinforces the importance of being physically active regardless of one's fitness level. Teachers without access to the software should administer these questions and then conduct a class discussion about the significance of the responses.

This chapter describes the physical activity questions and explains how to access this part of the assessment and incorporate it into the FitnessGram testing protocol. The chapter also addresses how a student's responses can be used to modify the prescriptive feedback provided to him or her.

DESCRIPTION OF ACTIVITY ASSESSMENT

The assessment includes three brief questions based on items from the Physical Activity Guidelines for Americans (HHS 2008). Each question asks students to report the number of days in a given week on which they performed certain forms of physical activity (aerobic, muscular strength, and bone strengthening). The following list shows the wording of the questions for activity areas of interest:

- **On how many of the past seven days did you participate in any aerobic physical activity for a total of 60 minutes or more over the course of a day?** This includes moderate activities as well as vigorous activities. Running, hopping, skipping, jumping rope, swimming, dancing, and bicycling are all examples of aerobic activities. (0, 1, 2, 3, 4, 5, 6, 7 days) _____

- **On how many of the past seven days did you do physical activity to strengthen or tone your muscles?** This includes exercises such as playing on playground equipment, climbing trees, and playing tug-of-war. Lifting weights and working with resistance bands are also muscle-strengthening activities. (0, 1, 2, 3, 4, 5, 6, 7 days) _____

- **On how many of the past seven days did you do physical activity to strengthen your bones?** This category includes exercises such as running, hopping, skipping, jumping rope, and dancing. (0, 1, 2, 3, 4, 5, 6, 7 days) _____

ADMINISTRATION

To increase the validity of the assessment, prepare your students ahead of time to answer the questions. Explain the different types of physical activity (aerobic, muscular strength, and bone strengthening) and illustrate (with examples) how to count the number of days of activity. This discussion might be conducted as part of an effort to teach children about how much physical activity they should try to do each week. The activity assessment may not be valid for children in grades K through 3 because young children may have difficulty in accurately recalling the information.

These questions can be administered to students in various ways; here are two suggested methods:

- Make copies of the Physical Activity Questions worksheet (figure 9.1), which is available in the web resource. This sheet can be used as a question

list and even as a place for students to record their answers if the teacher will be recording all scores on a class score sheet (figure 5.1c), which is available in the web resource.

- Students can also record their responses on a Personal Fitness Record, which is also available in the web resource (figure 5.1, a and b).

When using the FitnessGram software, you need to know the following:

- How to include the three questions—When creating a FitnessGram Test Event, you need to check the Activity Days box in order to include the three physical activity questions on that test event.

- How to record the results—When entering FitnessGram test scores, find the appropriate column and enter the number of activity days reported by the student.

If a child completes the FitnessGram physical activity questions, feedback provided by the teacher should include information about the child's fitness performance and about his or her level of physical activity. For example, if a child scores high on fitness but does not appear to be active, he or she should receive encouraging information about the need to stay active in order to maintain his or her fitness. Alternatively, a child who scores low on fitness but appears to be active should receive feedback encouraging him or her to keep up efforts to be physically active. Such information reinforces to children the importance of being physically active regardless of their fitness level. See chapter 10 for more information about interpreting FitnessGram results and for information about how these questions are used.

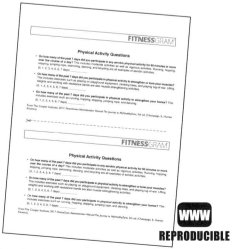

Figure 9.1 The Physical Activity Questions worksheet is available in the accompanying web resource.

KEY CONCEPTS

- Understand the importance of including the physical activity questions in the Fitness-Gram assessment.

- Recognize that a child's performance on physical fitness tests can be influenced by heredity, maturation, and body composition.

- Understand that giving students constructive feedback about their level of physical activity can be motivating.

- Before administering the questions, prepare students by explaining the different types of physical activity addressed (aerobic, muscular strength, and bone strengthening) and illustrate (with examples) how to count the number of days of activity.

Interpreting FitnessGram Results

FitnessGram uses criterion-referenced standards to evaluate fitness performance. The standards have been established to represent a level of fitness that is associated with reduced risk of obesity and other conditions associated with metabolic syndrome (i.e., conditions that result from sedentary living). Performance is classified into one of two general areas: the Healthy Fitness Zone or one of the Needs Improvement Zones. Attaining the Healthy Fitness Zone for a test indicates that the child has a sufficient fitness level to provide important health benefits. The Needs Improvement Zone should be interpreted as an indication that the child may be at risk if that level of fitness stays the same over time. In 2010, to refine the feedback provided to students, a third zone was developed for aerobic capacity and body composition: the Needs Improvement—Health Risk Zone. For more information about the 2010 standards, refer to the discussion of FitnessGram standards for aerobic capacity in chapter 6 and the discussion of body composition standards in chapter 7.

This chapter explains the establishment of the criterion-referenced standards for the various assessments, how fitness results can be influenced by maturation and development, and how to interpret test results in the various dimensions of fitness. Additional information about performance-based recognition can be found in chapter 3.

DERIVATION OF CRITERION-REFERENCED STANDARDS

Helping children understand and interpret Fitness-Gram results requires a basic understanding of how the standards are established. Unlike the percentile-based standards used in some fitness batteries, the criterion-referenced standards used in FitnessGram are anchored to an outcome with inherent meaning and importance. (Several slight adjustments have been made in the standards for $\dot{V}O_2$max and body composition since this manual was first published.)

Additional Resources

Additional information about the derivation of criterion-referenced standards can be found in the *FitnessGram/ActivityGram Reference Guide* (Plowman and Meredith 2013), which can be downloaded at www.cooperinstitute.org/reference-guide.

The aerobic capacity standards were established with the use of nationally representative data from the National Health and Nutrition Examination Surveys between 1999 and 2002 (NHANES). Data for low levels of aerobic capacity (measured with a submaximal clinical-exercise test) were associated with the presence of metabolic syndrome, which is a collection of factors associated with increased risk for diabetes and cardiovascular disease (including high triglycerides, high blood pressure, and high levels of circulating insulin). In contrast, numerous studies have documented physical fitness as providing protection against health risks, even among overweight youth. Studies have also shown that the benefits of physical fitness may be independent of physical activity. These findings support the importance of evaluating potential health risks resulting from low levels of fitness.

FitnessGram standards for aerobic capacity establish three zones based on potential risks for future health problems. The Healthy Fitness Zone was established by determining the level of fitness required for a low risk for future health problems. The Needs Improvement—Health Risk Zone defines levels of fitness that indicate potential health risks

(whether current or future). Youth between these two zones are classified into an intermediate zone referred to as the Needs Improvement Zone.

The aerobic capacity standards are based on estimated aerobic capacity. Each of the primary assessments estimates aerobic capacity, but differences in the tests and in the associated prediction equations can lead to differences in fitness classification depending on which test is used. Detailed information about the derivation of these standards is available in the chapter titled "Aerobic Capacity Assessments" in the *FitnessGram/ActivityGram Reference Guide* (Plowman and Meredith 2013).

Like the aerobic capacity standards, the body composition standards were established with the use of nationally representative data from NHANES between 1999 and 2004. As was also the case with aerobic capacity, data for body fat were associated with the presence of metabolic syndrome. Evidence from numerous epidemiological studies has documented that body fat levels and associated risk factors track throughout adolescence and into adulthood. Therefore, it is important to identify youth who may be at increased risk so that preventive or treatment programs can be initiated.

The body composition standards, like those for aerobic capacity, establish three zones based on potential risks for future health problems. The Healthy Fitness Zone was established by determining body fat values that indicate a low risk for potential health problems. The Needs Improvement—Health Risk Zone, in contrast, defines levels of body fatness that indicate a clear or substantial risk for future health problems. Youth between these two zones are classified into the intermediate Needs Improvement Zone; these youth are not considered to be at high risk but should be encouraged to keep working to reduce body fat until they reach the Healthy Fitness Zone. Because there are also risks associated with being too lean, FitnessGram classification options for body composition also include a fourth option, the Very Lean Zone.

The body fat standards were then equated to corresponding body mass index (BMI) values from the U.S. Centers for Disease Control and Prevention (CDC) to ensure good classification agreement between the body fat standards and the BMI standards. The two assessments are very different and cannot be expected to agree perfectly; however, the BMI standards can be interpreted in a manner that is similar to that just described for body fat standards. Therefore, the CDC's BMI standards have been adopted as the BMI standards in FitnessGram, thus enabling us to provide youth with consistent information from FitnessGram and the CDC growth charts commonly used by pediatricians. For additional information about the adoption of the CDC's BMI standards, refer to chapter 7. Detailed information about the derivation of the body fat and BMI standards is available in the chapter titled "Body Composition Assessment" in the *FitnessGram/ActivityGram Reference Guide* (Plowman and Meredith 2013).

Criterion-referenced standards are more difficult to establish for musculoskeletal fitness than for aerobic capacity or body composition because few immediate health risks are associated with poor musculoskeletal fitness. Although lack of strength, muscle endurance, and flexibility may increase the risk of injuries and back problems later in life, children are not as susceptible to these health problems. The delayed nature of these risks makes it more difficult to determine how much musculoskeletal fitness is needed in order to experience important health benefits. Therefore, the approach used for most of these test items is a "contrasting group methodology" for determining the amount of fitness that is possible in each test with a reasonable amount of training. In other words, comparing a trained group with an untrained group makes it possible to establish empirically based cut points anchored in training responses to exercise rather than in health outcomes.

The standards that define the Healthy Fitness Zone for boys and for girls are provided in tables 10.1 and 10.3, respectively. The PACER lap counts associated with the Healthy Fitness Zone for boys and for girls are provided in tables 10.2 and 10.4, respectively. All students should strive to achieve a score that places them in the Healthy Fitness Zone for their sex. It is even possible for some students to score above the Healthy Fitness Zone. However, though FitnessGram acknowledges such performances, it does not recommend this level of performance as an appropriate goal for all students. Even so, students who desire to achieve a high level of athletic performance may need to consider setting goals beyond the Healthy Fitness Zone. All students should receive any needed assistance in setting realistic goals; such help is more likely to be needed by younger students.

INFLUENCE OF BODY SIZE AND MATURITY ON FITNESS

Body size (consisting of height and weight) is somewhat related to physical fitness as measured by a combination of tests. This influence varies considerably across individuals and is especially apparent in two ways:

- Excess weight associated with fatness tends to have a negative influence on aerobic capacity and on performance in test items requiring the body to be lifted or moved (e.g., upper-body strength items).

- Variation in body size associated with maturity can influence fitness around the time of the adolescent growth spurt and sexual maturation. The timing of this period is determined largely by genetics in adequately nourished children and varies considerably across individuals. As a result, maturation level tends to vary greatly within a given age group of early-adolescent children.

Changes in body fatness and body size can exert major effects on performance in fitness tests. During the adolescent maturation process, boys typically experience a clear spurt of growth in muscle mass, strength, power, and endurance, as well as a decrease in subcutaneous fat on the arms and legs. In contrast, girls typically experience considerably smaller growth spurts in strength, power, and endurance and tend to accumulate body fat. In addition, during periods of rapid maturational change, children may experience an increase or decrease in their ability to perform certain test items that is completely independent of their level of physical activity.

INTERPRETING PERFORMANCE IN PHYSICAL FITNESS ASSESSMENTS

Even though FitnessGram assessments have good reliability and validity, test results should be used only as rough indicators. Fitness scores can be influenced by a number of factors, most of which lie beyond a child's control—for example, as just

Table 10.1 FitnessGram Standards for the Healthy Fitness Zone—Boys

Age (yrs.)	AEROBIC CAPACITY $\dot{V}O_2$MAX (ML·KG⁻¹·MIN⁻¹)			PERCENT BODY FAT				BODY MASS INDEX			
	PACER, one-mile run, walk test										
	NI—HRZ*	NIZ*	HFZ*	VLZ*	HFZ	NIZ	NI—HRZ	VLZ	HFZ	NIZ	NI—HRZ
5	Completion of test (lap count and time standards not recommended)			≤8.8	8.9–18.8	18.9–26.9	≥27.0	≤13.8	13.9–16.8	16.9–18.0	≥18.1
6				≤8.4	8.5–18.8	18.9–26.9	≥27.0	≤13.7	13.8–17.1	17.2–18.7	≥18.8
7				≤8.2	8.3–18.8	18.9–26.9	≥27.0	≤13.7	13.8–17.6	17.7–19.5	≥19.6
8				≤8.3	8.4–18.8	18.9–26.9	≥27.0	≤13.9	14.0–18.2	18.3–20.5	≥20.6
9				≤8.6	8.7–20.6	20.7–30.0	≥30.1	≤14.1	14.2–18.9	19.0–21.5	≥21.6
10	≤37.3	37.4–40.1	≥40.2	≤8.8	8.9–22.4	22.5–33.1	≥33.2	≤14.4	14.5–19.7	19.8–22.6	≥22.7
11	≤37.3	37.4–40.1	≥40.2	≤8.7	8.8–23.6	23.7–35.3	≥35.4	≤14.8	14.9–20.5	20.6–23.6	≥23.7
12	≤37.6	37.7–40.2	≥40.3	≤8.3	8.4–23.6	23.7–35.8	≥35.9	≤15.2	15.3–21.3	21.4–24.6	≥24.7
13	≤38.6	38.7–41.0	≥41.1	≤7.7	7.8–22.8	22.9–34.9	≥35.0	≤15.7	15.8–22.2	22.3–25.5	≥25.6
14	≤39.6	39.7–42.4	≥42.5	≤7.0	7.1–21.3	21.4–33.1	≥33.2	≤16.3	16.4–23.0	23.1–26.4	≥26.5
15	≤40.6	40.7–43.5	≥43.6	≤6.5	6.6–20.1	20.2–31.4	≥31.5	≤16.8	16.9–23.7	23.8–27.1	≥27.2
16	≤41.0	41.1–44.0	≥44.1	≤6.4	6.5–20.1	20.2–31.5	≥31.6	≤17.4	17.5–24.5	24.6–27.8	≥27.9
17	≤41.2	41.3–44.1	≥44.2	≤6.6	6.7–20.9	21.0–32.9	≥33.0	≤18.0	18.1–24.9	25.0–28.5	≥28.6
>17	≤41.2	41.3–44.2	≥44.3	≤6.9	7.0–22.2	22.3–35.0	≥35.1	≤18.5	18.6–24.9	25.0–29.2	≥29.3

Age (yrs.)	Curl-up (no. completed)	Trunk lift (in.)	90° push-up (no. completed)	Modified pull-up (no. completed)	Flexed arm hang (secs.)	Back-saver sit and reach (in.)	Shoulder stretch†
5	≥2	6–12	≥3	≥2	≥2	8	Healthy Fitness Zone = touching fingertips together behind the back on both the right and left sides.
6	≥2	6–12	≥3	≥2	≥2	8	
7	≥4	6–12	≥4	≥3	≥3	8	
8	≥6	6–12	≥5	≥4	≥3	8	
9	≥9	6–12	≥6	≥5	≥4	8	
10	≥12	9–12	≥7	≥5	≥4	8	
11	≥15	9–12	≥8	≥6	≥6	8	
12	≥18	9–12	≥10	≥7	≥10	8	
13	≥21	9–12	≥12	≥8	≥12	8	
14	≥24	9–12	≥14	≥9	≥15	8	
15	≥24	9–12	≥16	≥10	≥15	8	
16	≥24	9–12	≥18	≥12	≥15	8	
17	≥24	9–12	≥18	≥14	≥15	8	
>17	≥24	9–12	≥18	≥14	≥15	8	

*HFZ = Healthy Fitness Zone, NIZ = Needs Improvement Zone, NI—HRZ = Needs Improvement—Health Risk Zone, and VLZ = Very Lean Zone.

†This test is scored yes/no, and the performer must reach this distance on both the right and left sides to achieve the HFZ.

Table 10.2 PACER Laps Associated With the Healthy Fitness Zone—Boys

Age (yrs.)	20-meter laps	15-meter laps
5–9	Completion of test (lap count and time standards not recommended)	
10	≥17	≥22
11	≥20	≥26
12	≥23	≥30
13	≥29	≥38
14	≥36	≥47
15	≥42	≥55
16	≥47	≥61
17	≥50	≥65
>17	≥54	≥70

Table 10.3 FitnessGram Standards for the Healthy Fitness Zone—Girls

Age (yrs.)	AEROBIC CAPACITY VO₂MAX (ML·KG⁻¹·MIN⁻¹) PACER, one-mile run, walk test			PERCENT BODY FAT				BODY MASS INDEX			
	NI—HRZ*	NIZ*	HFZ*	VLZ*	HFZ	NIZ	NI—HRZ	VLZ	HFZ	NIZ	NI—HRZ
5	Completion of test (lap count and time standards not recommended)			≤9.7	9.8–20.8	20.9–28.3	≥28.4	≤13.5	13.6–16.8	16.9–18.4	≥18.5
6				≤9.8	9.9–20.8	20.9–28.3	≥28.4	≤13.4	13.5–17.2	17.3–19.1	≥19.2
7				≤10.0	10.1–20.8	20.9–28.3	≥28.4	≤13.5	13.6–17.9	18.0–20.1	≥20.2
8				≤10.4	10.5–20.8	20.9–28.3	≥28.4	≤13.6	13.7–18.6	18.7–21.1	≥21.2
9				≤10.9	11.0–22.6	22.7–30.7	≥30.8	≤13.9	14.0–19.4	19.5–22.3	≥22.4
10	≤37.3	37.4–40.1	≥40.2	≤11.5	11.6–24.3	24.4–32.9	≥33.0	≤14.2	14.3–20.3	20.4–23.5	≥23.6
11	≤37.3	37.4–40.1	≥40.2	≤12.1	12.2–25.7	25.8–34.4	≥34.5	≤14.6	14.7–21.2	21.3–24.6	≥24.7
12	≤37.0	37.1–40.0	≥40.1	≤12.6	12.7–26.7	26.8–35.4	≥35.5	≤15.1	15.2–22.1	22.2–25.7	≥25.8
13	≤36.6	36.7–39.6	≥39.7	≤13.3	13.4–27.7	27.8–36.2	≥36.3	≤15.6	15.7–22.9	23.0–26.7	≥26.8
14	≤36.3	36.4–39.3	≥39.4	≤13.9	14.0–28.5	28.6–36.7	≥36.8	≤16.1	16.2–23.6	23.7–27.6	≥27.7
15	≤36.0	36.1–39.0	≥39.1	≤14.5	14.6–29.1	29.2–37.0	≥37.1	≤16.6	16.7–24.3	24.4–28.4	≥28.5
16	≤35.8	35.9–38.8	≥38.9	≤15.2	15.3–29.7	29.8–37.3	≥37.4	≤17.0	17.1–24.8	24.9–29.2	≥29.3
17	≤35.7	35.8–38.7	≥38.8	≤15.8	15.9–30.4	30.5–37.8	≥37.9	≤17.4	17.5–24.9	25.0–29.9	≥30.0
>17	≤35.3	35.4–38.5	≥38.6	≤16.4	16.5–31.3	31.4–38.5	≥38.6	≤17.7	17.8–24.9	25.0–29.9	≥30.0

Age (yrs.)	Curl-up (no. completed)	Trunk lift (in.)	90° push-up (no. completed)	Modified pull-up (no. completed)	Flexed arm hang (sec.)	Back-saver sit and reach (in.)	Shoulder stretch†
5	≥2	6–12	≥3	≥2	≥2	9	Healthy Fitness Zone = touching fingertips together behind the back on both the right and left sides.
6	≥2	6–12	≥3	≥2	≥2	9	
7	≥4	6–12	≥4	≥3	≥3	9	
8	≥6	6–12	≥5	≥4	≥3	9	
9	≥9	6–12	≥6	≥4	≥4	9	
10	≥12	9–12	≥7	≥4	≥4	9	
11	≥15	9–12	≥7	≥4	≥6	10	
12	≥18	9–12	≥7	≥4	≥7	10	
13	≥18	9–12	≥7	≥4	≥8	10	
14	≥18	9–12	≥7	≥4	≥8	10	
15	≥18	9–12	≥7	≥4	≥8	12	
16	≥18	9–12	≥7	≥4	≥8	12	
17	≥18	9–12	≥7	≥4	≥8	12	
>17	≥18	9–12	≥7	≥4	≥8	12	

*HFZ = Healthy Fitness Zone, NIZ = Needs Improvement Zone, NI—HRZ = Needs Improvement—Health Risk Zone, and VLZ = Very Lean Zone.

†Test is scored yes/no; must reach this distance on right and left sides to achieve the HFZ.

Table 10.4 PACER Laps Associated With the Healthy Fitness Zone—Girls

Age (yrs.)	20-meter laps	15-meter laps
5–9	Completion of test (lap count and time standards not recommended)	
10	≥17	≥22
11	≥20	≥26
12	≥23	≥30
13	≥25	≥32
14	≥27	≥35
15	≥30	≥39
16	≥32	≥42
17	≥35	≥46
>17	≥38	≥49

discussed, maturation and development. A child's fitness level and response to training are also determined to a great degree by his or her genetics; for instance, some children improve performance more rapidly than others, and some can perform at much higher levels than others regardless of training. Therefore, rather than emphasizing a child's fitness scores, it is more important to emphasize his or her involvement in regular physical activity. Good physical fitness holds little value if it is not maintained through continued involvement in physical activity.

The FitnessGram Student Report provides personalized feedback that can help a child (as well as his or her parents) become more informed about levels of health-related fitness. The sample report presented in figure 10.1 highlights some of the format's features. As is evident in the illustration, the report uses easy-to-read bar charts to indicate fitness levels for each completed test. In addition, comparisons between past performance and current test results allow for some indication of trends over time.

Personalized messages appear in the text blocks to provide students with individualized feedback, which is generated by algorithms in the software that take into account a child's overall fitness profile. Students with favorable scores on the assessments (i.e., those who reach the Healthy Fitness Zone) receive congratulatory messages and reminders to maintain their involvement in physical activity. Students with less favorable scores (i.e., those in one of the Needs Improvement Zones) receive supportive messages and prescriptive feedback about how to be more active and how to improve their scores. If scores are entered for more than one assessment in a given fitness area, the best performance is printed.

If the FitnessGram physical activity questions are completed (see chapter 9), the individualized feedback provided on the FitnessGram Report factors in the child's responses to the physical activity questions. This feature allows the child to receive positive encouragement for being active even if he or she is not in the Healthy Fitness Zone. It also provides clear indications to children who are already fit that it is important for them to remain active. The general content of the integrated feedback about fitness and activity is illustrated in the conceptual matrix presented in table 10.5. The

actual feedback is both more detailed and specific to each dimension of fitness (i.e., aerobic capacity, musculoskeletal fitness, and body composition), but this chart illustrates the general concept. Given the power of this integrated feedback, the physical activity questions, though optional, are strongly recommended. If children do not complete the questions, then the feedback is based only on their fitness scores, which can send the wrong message.

If the physical activity questions are administered, responses can be evaluated with reference to the Physical Activity Guidelines for Americans (HHS 2008) issued by the U.S. Department of Health and Human Services to determine whether a given student is engaging in adequate levels of physical activity. Children and adolescents aged 6 to 17 years should engage in 60 minutes or more of physical activity per day, including the following kinds of activity:

- Aerobic—The 60 minutes or more per day should involve mostly either moderate- or vigorous-intensity aerobic activity and should include vigorous-intensity activity on at least three days per week.

- Muscle strengthening—Part of the 60 minutes or more of daily activity should include muscle-strengthening activity on at least three days per week.

- Bone strengthening—Part of the 60 minutes or more of daily activity should include bone-strengthening activity on at least three days per week.

Because the different dimensions of fitness are influenced by different factors, the following sections provide specific information about how each dimension should be interpreted and how it can be improved.

Aerobic Capacity

Aerobic capacity is the ability of the respiratory, cardiovascular, and muscular systems to take up, transport, and use oxygen during exercise and activity. The best measure of aerobic capacity is generally a laboratory measure of $\dot{V}O_2$max. FitnessGram output for this area of fitness is the calculated score for aerobic capacity, which can be used in comparing

FitnessGram Student Report

Joe Smith (ID:829202044)

Grade: 5 (Age: 11)

Teacher: Jogger, Jane

School: Cooper Elementary

District: Cooper District

Report Date: 5/10/2016

	Past	Current
Test Date:	11/3/2015	5/1/2016
Height:	5' 6"	5' 6"
Weight	125 lbs	124 lbs

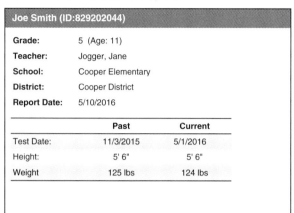

Aerobic Capacity

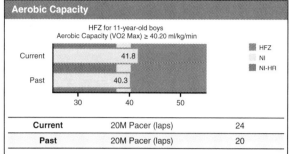

Current	20M Pacer (laps)	24
Past	20M Pacer (laps)	20

Congratulations! Your aerobic capacity is in the Healthy Fitness Zone and you are physically active most days. To maintain health and fitness, continue to participate in physical activities for at least 60 minutes each day. Keep your Body Mass Index (BMI) in the Healthy Fitness Zone.

Musculoskeletal Fitness

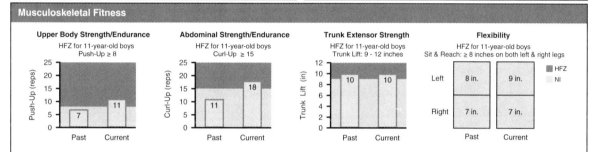

Your abdominal, trunk, and upper-body strength are all in the Healthy Fitness Zone. To maintain your fitness, be sure that your strength-training activities include exercises for all of these areas. Strength activities should be done at least 3 days per week.

In addition to aerobic and muscle-strengthening activities, it is important to perform stretching exercises to maintain or improve flexibility and some weight-bearing activity (e.g. running, hopping, jumping or dancing) to ensure good bone health at least 3 days per week.

Body Composition

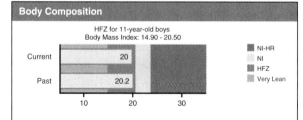

Good news! Your body composition is in the Healthy Fitness Zone. To maintain this healthy level of body composition, remember to:
-Be active for at least 60 minutes every day.
-Limit screen time to less than 2 hours a day.
-Make healthy food choices including fresh fruits and vegetables.
-Limit fried foods, foods with added sugars and sugary drinks.

Physical Activity

Reported Activity/Past 7 Days	Days	Goal
Aerobic activity for a total of 60 minutes or more	7	7
Muscle strengthening activity	3	3
Bone strengthening activity	2	3

To be healthy and fit, it is important to do some physical activity for a total of 60 minutes or more daily. Aerobic exercise is good for your heart and body composition. Muscular and bone-strengthening exercises are good for your muscles and joints.Congratulations! You are doing aerobic activity most or all days and muscular-strengthening exercises. Add some bone-strengthening exercises to improve your overall fitness.

HFZ: Healthy Fitness Zone; NI: Needs Improvement; NI-HR: Needs Improvement - Health Risk

FitnessGram.net

Figure 10.1 Sample FitnessGram Student Report from the FitnessGram software.

Table 10.5 Conceptual Matrix Used to Integrate Fitness and Activity Results

	PHYSICALLY ACTIVE?	
Fitness results	**Yes**	**No**
Scores in Healthy Fitness Zone	Congratulations. You are in the Healthy Fitness Zone. You are doing regular physical activity, and this is keeping you fit.	Congratulations. You are in the Healthy Fitness Zone. To keep fit, it is important that you do regular physical activity.
Scores not in Healthy Fitness Zone	Even though your scores were not in the Healthy Fitness Zone, you are doing regular physical activity. Keep up the good work.	Your scores were not in the Healthy Fitness Zone. Try to increase your activity levels to improve your fitness and health.

performance either from one test date to another or between different test items. A low score on the aerobic field test may be influenced by many factors, including the following:

- Actual aerobic capacity level
- Body composition
- Running and walking efficiency and economy
- Motivation level during the testing experience
- Extreme environmental conditions
- Ability to pace oneself during the one-mile run or the walk test
- Genetics and innate ability

Changes in any of these factors can influence the test score.

Aerobic capacity can be improved substantially in an unconditioned person who begins participating regularly in sustained activities involving large muscle groups. The amount of improvement relates to the individual's beginning level of fitness and to the intensity, duration, and frequency of the training. The major portion of the improvement occurs during the first six months; thereafter, improvement is much slower.

Test results can also be influenced by changes brought on by maturation. For boys, aerobic capacity in relation to body weight stays relatively constant during the growing years. For girls, however, aerobic capacity tends to remain constant between ages 5 and 10 years but decreases thereafter due to increasing sex-specific essential fat.

Running economy also influences absolute performance. In boys, for example, test scores for the one-mile run tend to improve with age—even though $\dot{V}O_2max$ as expressed in relation to body weight tends to remain constant—because running economy improves. In 10- to 12-year-old girls, these field-test scores also tend to improve as the result of improved running economy; between ages 12 and 18, however, girls' scores tend to remain relatively constant because improved running economy is offset by declining $\dot{V}O_2max$ as expressed in relation to body weight.

The differences in age-related changes in the relation of running economy to test scores in the one-mile run or PACER test are taken into account when the scores are converted to estimated $\dot{V}O_2max$ by equations in the FitnessGram software. Instructors who do not use the FitnessGram software can calculate $\dot{V}O_2max$ by using the FitnessGram Score Sheet calculator (spreadsheet), which is available at www.pyfp.org. Students who do not achieve the Healthy Fitness Zone should be encouraged to establish physical activity goals that will help them improve their aerobic capacity.

Because aerobic capacity criterion standards are not available for students in grades K through 3, feedback is not provided for children in these grades. The aerobic capacity test recommended for these students is the PACER, and the object of the test for these younger students is simply to participate and to try to complete as many laps as possible. The main goal is to provide these students with the opportunity to have a positive experience with the PACER assessment. Nine-year-olds in grade 4 may receive a score evaluated against the criterion standard established for 10-year-olds; all 10-year-old students receive a score regardless of grade level.

Body Composition

Body composition standards have been established for percent body fat as measured through bioelectrical impedance analysis or calculated from skinfold measurement of the triceps and calf areas (and, for college students, the abdominal area). They have also been established for BMI as calculated from measurements of weight and height. The standards for the Healthy Fitness Zone fall between the Very Lean and Needs Improvement Zones. Students whose scores fall either below or above the Healthy Fitness Zone should receive appropriate attention because they have greater potential than others do to develop health problems related to their level of fatness or leanness.

Tables 10.1 and 10.3 indicate the Healthy Fitness Zone, Needs Improvement Zone, Needs Improvement—Health Risk Zone, and Very Lean Zone for both percent body fat and BMI. Students in the Needs Improvement Zone should work to move into the Healthy Fitness Zone because their body composition puts them at risk of developing health problems. Students in the Needs Improvement—Health Risk Zone must be strongly encouraged to modify their activity and eating behaviors in order to begin reducing their weight. Students in this category have a greater possibility of developing health problems, both now and in the future, if their body composition does not change.

When interpreting body composition scores, remember the following points:

- Skinfold measurements provide an estimate of body fatness.
- The skinfold method has a margin of error of 3 percent to 5 percent.
- BMI provides an estimate of the appropriateness of weight for height.
- Because BMI does *not* take into account muscle mass, some children with a high level of muscle mass (i.e., athletic build) may receive a score indicating that they are overweight or in the Needs Improvement Zone when in fact their body composition is healthy.

In general, students who score in the Needs Improvement Zone should be encouraged to work toward the Healthy Fitness Zone by slowly changing their body weight through increased physical activity and decreased consumption of high-calorie, low-nutrient food. Changing one's dietary and exercise habits can be very difficult, and students with severe obesity or an eating disorder may need professional assistance in their attempts to modify their behaviors. Evidence clearly indicates that in adults the health risks associated with obesity are moderated by participation in regular physical activity (HHS 1998). Because this relationship likely holds true for children as well, the emphasis for overweight children should be placed not on absolute weight or fat loss but on being physically active.

When interpreting body composition results, keep in mind the fact that most students whose results fall in the Needs Improvement Zone may have performances outside the Healthy Fitness Zone in other areas as well. If they improve their body composition, they will generally also improve their performance in aerobic capacity and muscular strength and endurance, especially in the upper body, due to a reduction in excess weight.

FitnessGram also identifies students who are exceptionally lean. A score in the Very Lean Zone is treated as being in the Healthy Fitness Zone in the output of the FitnessGram Report, but students in the Very Lean range receive a message indicating that being this lean may not be best for health. Parents and teachers should notice students who are categorized as Very Lean and should consider factors that may be responsible for their low level of body fat. Many students are naturally very lean, but some have inappropriate nutritional patterns, and a relative few have eating disorders. One factor to consider is whether the student's level of fat has changed suddenly from within the optimal range to a level identified as very lean; severe changes may signal a potential problem. The primary purpose of identifying very lean students is to create awareness of their current status, and any changes in status should be monitored.

FitnessGram results can be very helpful in allowing students to follow changes in their level of body fat over time. Obesity is a health problem for both children and adults, and tracking studies reveal that overweight and obesity track from childhood to adolescence and from adolescence to adulthood. To reduce problems with weight later in life, the issue should be addressed early on, before unhealthy lifestyle patterns and physiological effects are firmly established.

Muscular Strength, Endurance, and Flexibility

Students who score poorly in one or more areas of muscular strength, muscular endurance, and flexibility should be encouraged to participate in calisthenics and other strengthening and stretching activities to develop those areas. It is also essential, however, to remember that physical fitness training is very specific and that the areas of the body being tested represent only a fraction of the total body. For instance, if an individual focuses on activities that develop the extensors of the arms without equal attention to the flexors of the arms, the individual will fail to accomplish the key objective, which is to develop a healthy musculoskeletal system overall.

Remember, we must have strength and flexibility in the muscles on both sides of every joint. Therefore, one useful activity for all students is to identify exercises that strengthen and stretch the muscles at every major joint of the trunk, upper body, and lower body. Special attention may be needed in cases of poor performance on the measures of abdominal strength and trunk extensor strength and flexibility. Gaining strength and flexibility in these areas may help prevent low-back pain, which affects millions of people, both young and old.

 KEY CONCEPTS

- FitnessGram uses criterion-referenced standards that classify students into the Healthy Fitness Zone or one of the Needs Improvement Zones.

  - Achievement of the Healthy Fitness Zone indicates that a child has sufficient fitness to experience important health benefits.

  - Classification in the Needs Improvement Zone or the Needs Improvement—Health Risk Zone indicates that the child may be at increased risk if that level of fitness stays the same.

- When interpreting FitnessGram results, and when framing student encouragement, use the Physical Activity Guidelines for Americans (HHS 2008). Children and adolescents should be physically active for 60 minutes or more per day. Students should be encouraged to set physical activity goals that will lead to the desired improvement in or maintenance of fitness performance.

  - Aerobic—Children and adolescents should be active every day for 60 minutes. A majority of this time should be spent in moderate- or vigorous-intensity physical activity and should be vigorous on at least three days per week (e.g., running, hopping, skipping, jumping rope, swimming, dancing, bicycling).

  - Muscle strengthening—Children and adolescents should perform muscle-strengthening activity on at least three days per week. This type of activity can be either structured (e.g., doing push-ups, curl-ups, and other calisthenics in physical education; lifting weights) or unstructured (e.g., playing on playground equipment, climbing trees, playing tug-of-war).

- Bone strengthening—Children and adolescents should perform bone-strengthening activity on at least three days per week. This type of activity produces force on the bones and promotes bone growth (e.g., running, jumping rope, hopping, and other activities that include these movements).

- Children and adolescents should be encouraged to participate in activities that are enjoyable, age appropriate, and varied in type.

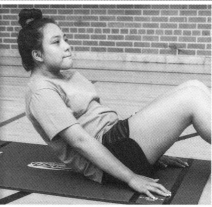

Understanding and Using FitnessGram Data

Perhaps the most influential step in the fitness assessment process is that of reporting fitness scores. "Purposeful measurement is an appropriate component of quality physical education. Combining fitness measurement and instruction is an appropriate instructional strategy and should be the main reason for measuring fitness. Measurement without a plan for using the data does little to serve students' needs and is not an educationally sound practice" (NASPE 2009, p. 2).

Understandably, stakeholders place great value in knowing how students score on fitness evaluations because student success is the ultimate measuring stick for evaluating effectiveness in any subject area. At the same time, this reality can create a dilemma for physical education teachers. If fitness scores are not viewed in the appropriate context, teachers may begin to "teach to the test," become frustrated with unmotivated students, or feel unsuccessful in terms of empowering student achievement. With these challenges in mind, this chapter provides you with appropriate strategies for reporting FitnessGram data (i.e., fitness scores) in ways that positively affect student learning, guide curriculum development, and inform parents and administrators of appropriate ways to interpret fitness data.

USING FORMATIVE AND SUMMATIVE ASSESSMENTS WITH FITNESSGRAM

Fitness data are used in a variety of ways depending on stakeholders' needs. Specifically, they are used at the student level to improve or maintain fitness; at the teacher level to guide curriculum and measure outcomes; and at the district, state, and national levels to determine overall fitness levels of large groups of students. When collecting and interpreting fitness data, two types of assessment are used: formative and summative.

Formative assessments are ongoing, and teachers use them to improve instructional methods and aid student learning. For example, if a physical education teacher observes that some students did not grasp a concept, she or he can incorporate a review activity or use an alternative instructional strategy when redelivering the concept. In this way, formative assessments are used throughout the school year to adjust and correct students' learning of skills and concepts. This process guides students in learning appropriate outcomes aligned with suitable objectives. For FitnessGram, examples of formative assessment include the following:

- Conducting pre-tests in each domain of learning (psychomotor, cognitive, affective)
- Quizzing students on concepts (e.g., contrasting muscular strength with muscular endurance)
- Observing students and providing feedback about correct form for the push-up
- Evaluating and modifying student-designed fitness goals
- Having students practice the curl-up assessment weekly in order to measure improvement

Summative assessments, on the other hand, are typically used to evaluate the effectiveness of instructional programs or to guide curriculum planning. The goal of summative assessment is to evaluate student competence in each domain of learning after an instructional phase is complete. For FitnessGram, examples of summative assessment include the following:

- A final exam covering health-related fitness knowledge
- Post-test on FitnessGram

- Comprehensive student fitness portfolio

Table 11.1 describes common FitnessGram reports that can be found in the reports section in the FitnessGram software. The table also provides an example of how each report can be used. FitnessGram reports serve as tangible reminders of what students learn and can do in class; they also provide teachers with a means for gaining parent, faculty, and administrative support for physical education and activity programs.

Teachers who do not have access to the FitnessGram software may send home a Personal Fitness Record (figure 5.1, *a* or *b*) for each student. These forms are included in the web resource, which also contains the forms for the FitnessGram Longitudinal Tracking Chart that students can use to graph their own scores over time (figure 11.1).

USING FITNESSGRAM DATA WITH STUDENTS

When teaching fitness, we must ask questions such as the following: What do we want students to learn and be able to do? How will we know if they have learned it? How can we help students get to where we want them to be? In general terms, as put forth in a position statement by the National Association for Sport and Physical Education (2003), high-quality physical education offers students opportunities to receive appropriate instruction and learn meaningful content. In terms of fitness in particular, the

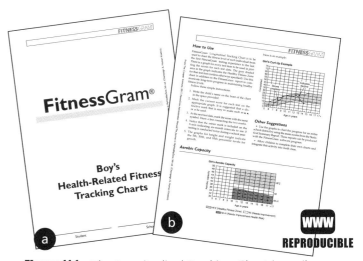

Figure 11.1 The Longitudinal Tracking Chart is available for *(a)* boys and *(b)* girls in the accompanying web resource.

position statement indicates that physical education should provide the following:

- Fitness education and assessment to help children understand and either improve or maintain their physical well-being
- Development of cognitive concepts related to motor skill and fitness
- Promotion of regular, appropriate physical activity both now and throughout life

- Regular assessment to monitor and reinforce student learning

In SHAPE America's national standards for physical education, standard 3 states, "The physically literate individual demonstrates the knowledge and skills to achieve and maintain a health-enhancing level of physical activity and fitness" (SHAPE America 2014). In other words, students should understand the components of health-related fitness

Table 11.1 Uses of Report Data in FitnessGram Reports

Report	Description	Uses
FitnessGram Report	Communicates results of fitness evaluation to students and parents. Evaluates performance against Healthy Fitness Zone (HFZ) standards. Provides suggestions for improving or maintaining fitness depending on student's performance.	Students—Develop short- and long-term fitness goals for academic year(s).
		Parents—Obtain information about child's fitness and strategies to help child improve or maintain.
		Teachers—Initiate communication with students and parents; follow up to encourage student and parents to be active at home.
FitnessGram Summary Report (Score)	Provides fitness scores for various selected groups of students, either for one or for multiple evaluation dates available from the database.	Teachers—Recognize areas of health-related fitness that have improved or need improvement by individual students or by class; focus lesson plans according to needs of each class.
		Campus administration—Recognize which teachers have conducted fitness testing and understand how many students have participated.
FitnessGram Summary Report (Presidential Youth Fitness Award, or PYFA)	Lists students who have achieved HFZ standards (can be designed to list all students who have passed a specific number of evaluation items).	Teachers—Use to aid lesson planning, quickly identify tests for which students achieved the HFZ, complete grant reports requiring class or school results, and prepare reports or awards (PYFA).
		Campus administration—Prepare summary reports regarding overall school achievement; initiate campus-wide activities based on specific fitness components.
FitnessGram Longitudinal Tracking Chart	Graphs all fitness scores for each evaluation item in the database for a given student (can track individual student's fitness level throughout the K-12 years).	Students, teachers, and parents—Track long-term performance of a student in each component of health-related fitness and monitor progress toward long-term goals.
FitnessGram Statistical Report	Contains group summary information, including mean, standard deviation, range of scores, and percentage of students achieving HFZ standards by test item, age, and sex.	Teachers—Recognize areas of HFZ achievement by sex, grade, and fitness component; use for lesson planning and preparing for education nights with parent and faculty groups.
		Campus administration—See the need for additional fitness equipment, teacher training, or education based on each fitness component; recognize HFZ achievement by sex and grade; view reports for one teacher or multiple teachers.
		District administration—Recognize HFZ achievement by grade and sex for reporting, training, and grant applications; view reports for one school or multiple schools.
FitnessGram Overview Report	Provides a graphic representation of HFZ achievement percentage for each fitness component. Shows aggregate data over time (current and past test events) and can be pulled by school(s), district(s), grade level, and HFZ achievement per test component(s).	Campus administration—See the need for additional fitness equipment, teacher training, or education based on fitness component, sex, or grade level.
		District administration—See the need for teacher training or high-level (district or state) support.
		Overall surveillance—Use for educational purposes, summary information, or documentation for grant funding.

Exporting Scores From FitnessGram Software

Many people want to use FitnessGram data for other purposes, such as comparing FitnessGram results with other student variables captured by the school district or state—for example, academic achievement, student absenteeism, and student discipline issues. To perform such analyses, users can export FitnessGram scores from the software. In addition to scores, the export file contains test-event dates, test items, the student's sex, and the student's age and grade at the time of the test event. Users who have a research partner with specific data needs or whose district prohibits exporting student information (e.g., name, ID number) can omit that information from the export. Specific steps for generating the Research Extract are provided in the help files of the FitnessGram software.

and how to evaluate their personal fitness levels. Ultimately, the objective is for students to learn self-measurement, which enables them to plan for personal fitness throughout life.

FitnessGram allows students to conduct self-measurement by accessing the software. The student report includes a custom message that summarizes the child's performance in each component of health-related fitness and provides suggestions, as appropriate, for maintaining or promoting good fitness; the suggestions are based on the student's fitness and activity levels. This information can be used to determine each individual's baseline fitness level and to encourage him or her to create appropriate SMART goals—that is, goals that are specific, measurable, attainable, realistic, and time specific—for fitness, nutrition, and lifestyle habits. Setting SMART goals puts students on a path to success; examples are provided in table 11.2.

To help with goal-setting activities, the accompanying web resource includes materials such as the following:

- Physical Activity Goals worksheet (figure 11.2)
- Get Fit Conditioning Program materials (figure 2.3, *a–c*), which help students create their own six-week fitness program to increase health-related fitness
- Personal Fitness Record (figure 5.1, *a* and *b*), which students can use to record results and reflect on their scores

When promoting physical activity with children and adolescents, be aware of the following factors that can affect their physical activity and fitness levels.

- Explaining long-term health benefits may not motivate students in this age group to participate in physical activity. Focus instead on how a

Table 11.2 Examples of SMART Goals and Ways to Reach Them

Goal	Ways to reach
By the end of _____ (semester or number of weeks), I will improve my aerobic-capacity assessment score by participating in vigorous activities on at least 3 days per week for 60 minutes per day. I will track my activity using an activity tracking log.	Do daily jogging and cross-training (e.g., elliptical, jumping jacks, burpees).
By the end of _____ (semester or number of weeks), I will improve my upper-body strength by doing _____ push-ups (begin with number performed in previous test and gradually increase each week) on at least 3 days per week. I will track my activity using an activity log.	Do strength training 3 times per week by lifting weights or using body weight.
By the end of _____ (semester or number of weeks), I will improve my core strength by doing _____ curl-ups and trunk extension exercises (begin with number performed in previous test and gradually increase each week) on at least 3 days per week. I will track my activity using an activity log.	Do abdominal-strength exercises 3 or 4 times per week (e.g., plank, side plank, crunch, reverse crunch, V-ups).
By the end of _____ (semester or number of weeks), I will have worked to improved my body composition by tracking my food consumption on a food tracking log. I will focus on portion sizes and reducing the number of sweetened beverages.	Track food and drink consumption, including portion size.

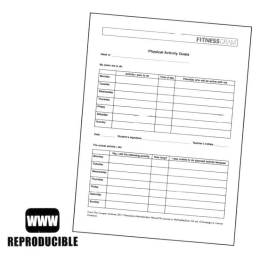

Figure 11.2 The Physical Activity Goals worksheet is available in the accompanying web resource.

student values an activity and on whether he or she feels competent and satisfied with it; these factors may exert more influence than health benefits do on the child's future participation.

- Families that are more physically active tend to have children who are more physically active and more competent in movement activities. In contrast, a sedentary family can negatively influence a child's motivation to participate in physical activity.

- A child's level of physical activity can also be influenced by environmental factors, such as neighborhood, climate, and access and transportation to community recreation areas (e.g., parks, pools, walking paths).

- A child's interest in physical activity and sport may change with age and may be influenced by peers.

When working with adolescents, be aware of the following unique factors that may affect students in this age group.

- Developmental changes can affect a student's functional abilities (e.g., muscular strength, speed, flexibility).

- Developmental and hormonal changes can affect a student's attitude about participating in physical activity. For example, developmental changes may leave a student feeling uncomfortable about sweating in front of peers or "dressing out" for physical education. Be sensitive to such concerns and establish a safe learning

environment to help students work through these developmental changes.

- As a student's responsibilities increase with age, time demands can make it difficult to engage in physical activity outside of the school day. For example, a teen may take on a job or begin helping out with additional household chores, either of which reduces the amount of time available for physical activity outside of school.

Understanding the unique needs of a given age group can help teachers work with students to positively influence their health-related fitness and promote lifelong physical activity.

Adolescents must also be taught the necessary skills to assume responsibility for their own personal fitness and enjoyment of physical activity. To this end, teachers should encourage and guide adolescents to apply their health-related fitness knowledge and their test results to endeavors such as creating a personal wellness plan and setting personal goals. Having students design their own fitness plans fosters enjoyment of physical activity for a lifetime and teaches management skills that are crucial to lifelong fitness. Students can have fun creating and carrying out their plans even as they demonstrate increasing responsibility for their choices. Before students are asked to create a fitness plan, they must be taught the basic concepts of the FITT principle (frequency, intensity, time, and type), as well as goal-setting skills. They must also be exposed to a variety of activities and learn to categorize them into the health-related component of fitness. To help students get started in creating their plans, refer to the Get Fit Conditioning Program in the web resource (figure 2.3, *a–c*).

Other developmentally appropriate activities are available to help students explore health-related fitness concepts and to help teachers address health-related fitness and promote lifelong physical activity. Examples include the Physical Best activity guides (SHAPE America 2011a, 2011b), as well as *Physical Education for Lifelong Fitness* (3rd edition) (SHAPE America 2011c) and *Fitness for Life* (Corbin and Le Masurier 2014).

USING FITNESSGRAM DATA WITH TEACHERS

In general, teachers use assessments to determine students' needs; more specifically, physical education teachers should analyze fitness data (using Fitness-Gram reports) when making curricular decisions. For example, if, after running the FitnessGram Summary Report (Score), a teacher sees that a *large* percentage of a class does not exhibit healthy levels of aerobic capacity, the teacher might consider revising his or her program to implement appropriate activities to increase students' aerobic capacity. If, on the other hand, a *smaller* percentage of the class fails to show healthy levels of aerobic capacity, then the teacher might instead use small-group, differentiated instruction for the students who need help.

Physical educators should also analyze the fitness levels of individual students. This analysis can be done quickly and efficiently by running the Fitness-Gram Summary Report (PYFA) or the Longitudinal Tracking Report. The reports should be used *not to grade students* but as an informational resource to guide instruction. For instance, a teacher can use report information to teach students how to set short- and long-term fitness goals. By using the available data to drive curricular decisions and teach students, a physical education teacher can feel confident in his or her efforts to improve student learning.

Here again, the Physical Best activity guides provide excellent resources for physical education teachers with respect to planning for health-related fitness. Physical Best is not a stand-alone curriculum; rather, it provides K-12 lessons to enable the integration of fitness-related concepts into an existing curriculum. Physical Best is aligned with the national standards for quality physical education (SHAPE America 2014) and teaches health-related fitness concepts through movement.

USING FITNESSGRAM DATA WITH PARENTS

Parents need to be aware of the value of physical fitness. To this end, the FitnessGram Report provides parents with information about the benefits of fitness, as well as their child's performance results on each health-related fitness evaluation. If a child has participated in the FitnessGram evaluation more than once, the parents will receive both past and current results; the report also suggests strategies, as needed, for maintaining or improving the child's fitness. When reports are distributed, teachers should make themselves available to speak with any parent who would like help with

FitnessGram Promotes Student Success
Spotlight on FitnessGram and ActivityGram

Susan Searls
Physical Education Teacher
Davenport School of the Arts, Polk County Schools, Florida

For me, the philosophy of FitnessGram and ActivityGram has always been student centered. It focuses on making it easy for my students to understand fitness concepts with hands-on practice and activities that help them achieve individual goals and understand the concept of lifetime fitness. As a physical education teacher, I have been using this program for more than 20 years, and although fitness trends have changed a great deal in that time, FitnessGram has remain focused on students' health-related fitness.

Over the years, students have become less and less interested in sport and fitness, but FitnessGram and ActivityGram provide tools to help students, parents, and school personnel understand what we can do to promote lifelong fitness. I send reports home twice per year, and I receive positive feedback from parents; in addition, the students enjoy logging their activity and tracking their progress from beginning to end.

For years, I have been using the PACER, as well as weekly practice activities for muscular strength, muscular endurance, and flexibility. When students finish an assessment, they write their scores in their individual log books. They keep these log books for all the years they are with me. One student came up to me after a first-semester PACER assessment, showed me his log book, and said, "Look, Coach—I improved my cardio fitness a lot this year." He then showed me his score from the first assessment, done the previous year, and compared it with his score from the current year. He had improved by 22 laps! I can't wait to see what he does by the end of this year.

FitnessGram and all of its resources allow me to individualize my instruction and assessment without a lot of extra work or record keeping. The FitnessGram reports enable me to promote health-related fitness with students, parents, fellow teachers, administrators, and the community at large. They also help me get the assistance and resources I need to keep motivating my students to achieve lifelong fitness. I believe this program has allowed me to continue teaching for my 26 years, and I still love to go to work every day because I know it makes a difference in my students' lives.

interpreting the results. By providing parents with personalized reports, teachers can enhance parental involvement in promoting and participating in physical activity for their child.

USING FITNESSGRAM DATA WITH ADMINISTRATORS

Teachers and administrators can use FitnessGram data in a variety of ways. For example, by analyzing school data, educators can determine areas of concentration and frame discussions about how to make instructional decisions to address areas of student need in the physical education program. If a majority of students achieve healthy levels of fitness, data can be used for the following:

- Highlighting the importance of physical education and physical activity programs

- Illustrating how curriculum planning and formative assessment have led to maintenance or improvement of student fitness levels

- Helping other schools that may be struggling with achieving healthy levels of student fitness

If a majority of students do *not* achieve healthy levels of fitness, data can be used for the following:

- Advocating for more time in physical education and physical activity programs

- Advocating for resources (e.g., professional development, equipment, additional personnel) to meet student needs

- Demonstrating the need to support joint-use policies, additional funding, and additional safe places to play through community partnerships

 KEY CONCEPTS

- Meet the responsibility of helping students improve so that they can achieve the Healthy Fitness Zone and of encouraging maintenance for students who already have healthy levels of fitness.

- Teach students about the fitness assessment process and how to interpret scores to encourage lifelong fitness using the following strategies:
  - SMART goals
  - Formative assessment (ongoing)
  - Summative assessment (evaluating student competence after instruction)

- Communicate fitness results to parents to inform them of their child's level of fitness and to help them learn about the benefits of being physically fit.

- Use reports from the FitnessGram software to communicate fitness data to administrators and to advocate for health-related physical fitness concepts.

PART III

ActivityGram
Assessment Module

ActivityGram is a behaviorally based activity assessment tool that can help young children and adolescents learn more about their physical activity habits. The assessment involves a three-day recall of the various activities performed. The predominant activity in each 30-minute block of time is coded, and the resulting data are used to determine the amount of time spent in activity, the times when a child is active or inactive, and the types of activity performed. Recommendations are based on the national guidelines published in the Physical Activity Guidelines for Americans (HHS 2008).

The ActivityGram module now includes two assessments: ActivityGram and ActivityGram Lite (Youth Activity Profile). ActivityGram Lite is a short survey inquiring about a student's physical activity at school and at home and about a student's sedentary activities. ActivityGram Lite was added to the ActivityGram module because it is a very time-efficient way to collect information about students' levels of physical activity.

Chapter 12 covers general principles for collecting accurate self-reported information about physical activity. Chapter 13 addresses ways to interpret ActivityGram and ActivityGram Lite test results.

ActivityGram
Administration

Because one major goal of physical education is to promote regular physical activity, the curriculum should include assessments of physical activity. If children are not physically active, they cannot maintain physical fitness. The ActivityGram physical activity recall assessment tool helps teachers offer instruction and feedback related to physical activity topics. In order to complete the assessment, children must be able to categorize different types of activity, describe the intensity of an activity, and estimate the length of time (duration) spent being physically active. The ActivityGram student report provides detailed information about the child's activity habits, as well as prescriptive feedback about how active he or she should be.

ActivityGram is designed to be conducted as an "event" that is similar in focus and structure to the FitnessGram assessments. Instructors are encouraged to allot time in the curriculum to teach concepts related to physical activity and to use this new evaluation tool. Because of the cognitive demands of recalling physical activity, it may be difficult for young children to get accurate results. For this reason, the ActivityGram module is recommended for children in grades 5 and higher. However, if it is used for educational purposes only—and if some training or assistance is provided—it should still be possible for slightly younger children (i.e., in grades 3 and 4) to obtain meaningful results.

In order to use ActivityGram, you must have access to the FitnessGram software and allow students to enter their own information. Teachers without access to the software will be unable to use this assessment.

This chapter describes the ActivityGram module and provides guidelines for administering the instrument in physical education classes. For more information about the reliability and validity of physical activity assessments, refer to the chapter titled "Physical Activity Assessment" (Welk, Mahar, and Morrow 2013) in the *FitnessGram/ActivityGram Reference Guide* (Plowman and Meredith 2013), which is available online at www.cooperinstitute.org/reference-guide.

DESCRIPTION OF ACTIVITYGRAM

The ActivityGram assessment is based conceptually on a validated physical activity instrument known as the Previous Day Physical Activity Recall (PDPAR) (Weston, Petosa, and Pate 1997). In the PDPAR assessment, the child is asked to report his or her activity levels for each 30-minute block of time during the day; the format accommodates both school and nonschool days. Each assessment covers the period beginning at 7 a.m. and ending at 11 p.m. For each 30-minute block, the child is asked to report the predominant activity for that interval.

To facilitate useful responses, the ActivityGram assessment provides children with a list of common activities, which are divided into categories based on the Physical Activity Pyramid (figure 1.1): lifestyle activity, aerobic activity, aerobic sport, muscular activity, flexibility, and rest. The pyramid provides a useful way to describe the variety of physical activities that contribute to good health. Level 1 of the pyramid includes lifestyle activities, or activities that can be done as part of daily living (e.g., walking to school, riding a bike, raking leaves, and engaging in general outdoor play of all kinds). Level 2 contains a variety of aerobic activities, level 3 the aerobic sports, level 4 muscle fitness activities, level 5 flexibility, and level 6 resting activities (e.g., homework, TV viewing, eating). Children need to be able to categorize their activities in order to increase their involvement in healthy physical activity and minimize the amount of free time they spend in inactive pursuits.

For each activity selected in the assessment, students are asked to rate the intensity as Light, Moderate, or Vigorous. These descriptors were selected for consistency with current physical activity guidelines that describe recommended levels of moderate and vigorous physical activity.

After selecting an intensity, students are asked to specify the duration of the activity by indicating whether they were active in this activity for "all of the time" in the specified interval, "most of the time," or just for "some of the time." This approach allows each interval to be represented as three 10-minute bouts rather than one 30-minute bout. Students should pick "some of the time" if active for 1 to 10 minutes; "most of the time" if active for 11 to 29 minutes; or "all of the time" if active for 30 minutes. This distinction improves the accuracy of the assessment and reinforces to the child that

activity does not have to be continuous or done for long periods of time in order to be meaningful.

If a child selects an activity from the *rest* category, then the duration of the activity is assumed to be 30 minutes; that is, a student cannot select "some of the time" or "most of the time" for *rest* because students who were resting for only a portion of the time should also indicate what other type of activity they were performing in that time interval.

ACTIVITYGRAM ADMINISTRATION

ActivityGram is accessed through the software, and, as mentioned earlier, it is designed to be administered as an "event" similar in scope to FitnessGram. Teachers typically spend several weeks preparing for and completing the various fitness assessments, and this same level of attention should be devoted to administering the ActivityGram assessment. When this module is established as an important part of the curriculum, children put a better effort into it. Once a student has completed his or her ActivityGram tracking log, the student may access the software online with instructions provided by the teacher. Student involvement—as well as the accuracy of the assessment—can be enhanced by enlisting parents' help in reminding children to complete their daily activity logs. The web resource includes a file with an introductory letter, an instruction sheet, a sample activity log, and blank activity logs for days 1, 2, and 3 (figure 12.1).

It is inherently challenging to obtain accurate information about physical activity through self-report instruments, and the challenges are magnified in assessments with children. To address these challenges, the ActivityGram software provides an intuitive computer interface and some built-in aids to facilitate the child's recall of physical activity. However, before data collection takes place, children should be taught about the different types and intensities of physical activity to help them accurately distinguish the activities in which they engage. A sample protocol is included later in this chapter; it provides only a rough outline of how the instrument can be introduced, and further refinement or customization may be needed. This type of instruction enhances the educational value of the ActivityGram assessment and improves the accuracy of the results.

Most teachers give students the opportunity to practice fitness assessments before testing occurs,

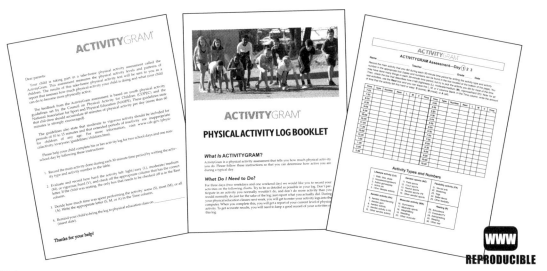

Figure 12.1 An ActivityGram assessment packet is available in the accompanying web resource.

and this approach is advisable for activity assessments as well. To help you facilitate this type of practice during a portion of a physical education class, a sample logging page is included in the web resources (figure 12.1). We recommended having all students briefly complete this practice log before they complete the ActivityGram for the first time. The following protocol can be used to instruct students about how to complete the practice log.

> To practice learning about activity, I would like to have you try to remember what you did yesterday after school. Think back to yesterday and write down the main activity that you did for each 30-minute period after school. You can write the name of the activity in the space or use the chart at the bottom of the page to write down the number. For each activity, estimate the intensity as either rest, light, moderate, or vigorous. (Help students select activities from the pyramid and rate the intensity of their activities.)

Although the instrument is intended to be a "recall" of the previous day's activity, accuracy may be improved by having children complete a detailed activity log during the day. The use of a log may not be necessary if the children are recalling only one day back in time, but it is strongly recommended for extended days of recall. ActivityGram assessment logs are included in the web resource (figure 12.1). Providing information to parents on a cover letter with the assessment log form helps promote parental involvement and support and provides a

reminder to children to actually complete the log. A sample parent letter is included in the web resource (figure 12.1). Requiring the completion of the log as a "participation activity" (i.e., as homework) is another way to promote compliance with the monitoring protocol.

The child must complete all three days of the assessment in order for the resulting ActivityGram report to print. The report includes information about the amount of activity performed, activity patterns during the day, and the types of activity performed as classified into the categories of the ActivityGram Physical Activity Pyramid. To find out how results are compiled and summarized, consult chapter 13.

A sample protocol for integrating ActivityGram into your classroom is presented in figure 12.2.

ACTIVITYGRAM LITE (YOUTH ACTIVITY PROFILE)

ActivityGram Lite is a short survey that asks students a series of questions reflecting on their physical activity before, during, and after school. ActivityGram Lite is based on the Youth Activity Profile, which was developed in 2012 at Iowa State University by Dr. Greg Welk. The purpose of developing ActivityGram Lite was to provide a physical activity assessment that did not require as much time to administer as ActivityGram. Once the survey is completed, students are shown their

Figure 12.2   Sample Training Protocol for Instruction on ActivityGram

Orientation to ActivityGram

Over the next few days, you are going to learn about the types and amounts of physical activity that you do in a normal day. Although you get some activity in physical education, you probably do a lot of other activities after school or at home. The ActivityGram assessment that we will do will allow you to track the different activities that you do over three different days: two days during the week and one weekend day. You will need to record the main activity that you do for each 30-minute block of time during the day. While you may do several activities, you will need to record only the main activity that you do during each block of time. The activities will be selected using the ActivityGram Physical Activity Pyramid (describe the pyramid using figure 1.1 in the web resource). For each activity, you will rate the intensity of the activity as either rest, light, moderate, or vigorous and then specify how long you did it.

Explanation About Physical Activity

Physical activity refers to movements that require the use of large muscle groups (arms and legs) and increase sweating and breathing rates. (Discuss examples of physical activity.) There are also a lot of different resting activities that might be done during the day. (Discuss examples of things that can be done during rest or while relaxing.) The ActivityGram Physical Activity Pyramid provides a way to categorize the different types of activity that you do. Descriptions of the different physical activities include the following types:

- Lifestyle activities are part of a normal day; examples include walking, bike riding, playing, housework, and yardwork.

- Aerobic activities are done to improve aerobic fitness; examples include jogging, bike riding, swimming, and dancing.

- Aerobic sports are sports that involve a lot of movement; they may be done with a few people or as part of a team, and they include field sports, court sports, and racquet sports.

- Muscular activities require a lot of strength—for example, gymnastics, cheer, dance and drill teams, track and field, weightlifting, calisthenics, wrestling, and martial arts.

- Flexibility activities involve stretching muscles as in martial arts (such as tai chi), stretching, yoga, and ballet.

If you do an activity that is not listed, you should pick the category that it belongs in and choose the "other" option provided in each category. (Discuss other activities not on the list.) For example if you were riding in a car, what type of activity would that be? (Other—rest.) If you were climbing trees, what might you select? (Other—muscular.) If you were just playing around the house, the activity might involve several different movements, but you would probably just select "other—lifestyle." Remember that most activities you do are probably "light" or "rest." You might only have a few periods each day when you are running or playing a bit harder.

Explanation About Intensity

Activities can be done at different intensities. Descriptions of the different intensities include the following: rest, light, moderate, and vigorous.

- *Rest* can be used to describe an activity that mostly involves sitting or standing but little motion.

- *Light* can be used to describe an activity that involves slow movements but is not too tiring.

- *Moderate* can be used to describe an activity that is between light and vigorous (such as brisk walking); it causes some increase in your breathing rate but is not too difficult.
- *Vigorous* can be used to describe an activity that involves quick movements and makes you breathe hard.

Explanation About Duration

Activity can be done for various periods of time. For example, you might be active for a few minutes and then rest for a few minutes. In fact, this is a good way to stay active throughout the day. You will pick the main activity that you do in each 30-minute period. The 30-minute time periods should be divided into three 10-minute bouts. Here are descriptions of the different durations.

- Movements performed for the entire 30 minutes: "all of the time" (all 30 minutes)
- Movements performed for at least two 10-minute bouts: "most of the time" (11 to 29 minutes)
- Movements performed for only one 10-minute bout: "some of the time" (1 to 10 minutes)

---

results in a report format. ActivityGram Lite is a quick assessment of the student's physical activity level and sedentary habits that can be used to help students set personal goals for physical activity. A copy of ActivityGram Lite is included in the web resource (figure 12.3).

Teachers without access to the FitnessGram application can have students complete the ActivityGram Lite survey and reflect on their responses afterward. However, it would be very difficult to provide students with any type of report.

Figure 12.3 The survey from ActivityGram Lite is included in the accompanying web resource.

Success With ActivityGram at El Paso Independent School District

Spotlight on FitnessGram and ActivityGram

Don Disney
Former Director of Health and Wellness
El Paso Independent School District (ISD), Texas

ActivityGram pre- and post-assessments are the first steps toward empowering students to change their behavior. These steps were taken in the El Paso ISD through the three-day ActivityGram recall. Every student taking physical education in grades 3 through 12 was required to perform a pre-ActivityGram and a post-ActivityGram as homework assignments through the web-based version of FitnessGram. Students without access to the Internet were provided with opportunities to complete the assignment before or after school in the computer lab.

The pre-ActivityGram was followed by a class discussion and a goal-setting assignment that included a simple action plan. Each student was provided with a worksheet and assigned a grade for completing the assignment, which included the short analysis, realistic goal setting, and an action plan. After students completed the assignment, the teacher delivered a summary lesson that motivated students to follow-up on their goals and implement the simple action plan. The teacher set up the post-ActivityGram event late in the spring semester, and the students completed the assignment as homework.

KEY CONCEPTS

- The ActivityGram physical activity recall provides a tool that helps teachers offer effective instruction and feedback related to physical activity topics.

  - The student is asked to report activity levels in 30-minute blocks during the day.

  - The recall covers the student's activity between 7 a.m. and 11 p.m. on two school days and one nonschool day.

  - The student categorizes each activity as lifestyle activity, aerobic activity, aerobic sport, muscular activity, flexibility activity, or rest activity.

  - Students rate the intensity of each activity as rest, light, moderate, or vigorous.

  - Students indicate the duration of the activity as all of the time, most of the time, or some of the time during the indicated time interval.

- ActivityGram is accessed through the FitnessGram software. Although this is a "recall" of the previous day's activity, accuracy may be improved by having children complete a detailed activity log before going to the computer lab.

- ActivityGram Lite (Youth Activity Profile) is a quick survey that can be used to determine a student's level of physical activity; it is available in the FitnessGram application. The ActivityGram Lite may be used when a teacher wants to spend less time administering the ActivityGram assessment.

- Activity tracking is essential to the process of teaching students about their physical activity levels and helping them learn to set effective goals.

Interpreting and Using ActivityGram Results

13

The ActivityGram physical activity recall provides detailed information about a child's physical activity patterns. Once the child completes the three days of assessment, the results are summarized and printed on the ActivityGram Report. The report includes information about the amount of activity performed, activity patterns throughout the day, and the types of activity performed; for a sample report, see figure 13.1.

The criterion-referenced standards used to determine the feedback provided in ActivityGram reports are based on the Physical Activity Guidelines for Americans (HHS 2008). These guidelines specify that children should perform a variety of activities and that the typical intermittent activity patterns of children should be encouraged. The guidelines are summarized in chapter 3 of this manual.

ActivityGram Student Report

ACTIVITY GRAM®

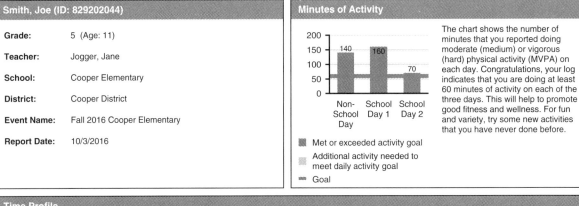

Smith, Joe (ID: 829202044)

Grade:	5 (Age: 11)
Teacher:	Jogger, Jane
School:	Cooper Elementary
District:	Cooper District
Event Name:	Fall 2016 Cooper Elementary
Report Date:	10/3/2016

Minutes of Activity

The chart shows the number of minutes that you reported doing moderate (medium) or vigorous (hard) physical activity (MVPA) on each day. Congratulations, your log indicates that you are doing at least 60 minutes of activity on each of the three days. This will help to promote good fitness and wellness. For fun and variety, try some new activities that you have never done before.

- Met or exceeded activity goal
- Additional activity needed to meet daily activity goal
- Goal

Time Profile

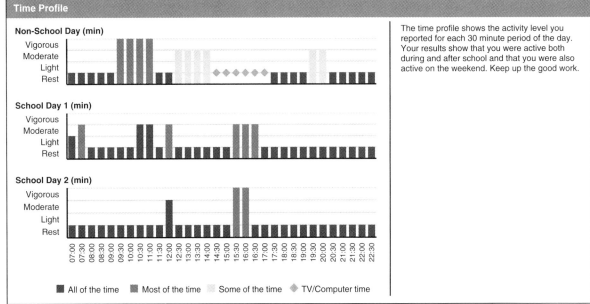

The time profile shows the activity level you reported for each 30 minute period of the day. Your results show that you were active both during and after school and that you were also active on the weekend. Keep up the good work.

■ All of the time ■ Most of the time ▨ Some of the time ◆ TV/Computer time

Activity Pyramid Profile

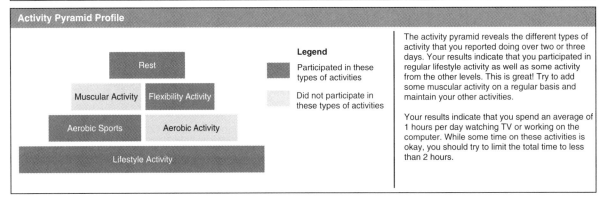

Legend

- Participated in these types of activities
- Did not participate in these types of activities

The activity pyramid reveals the different types of activity that you reported doing over two or three days. Your results indicate that you participated in regular lifestyle activity as well as some activity from the other levels. This is great! Try to add some muscular activity on a regular basis and maintain your other activities.

Your results indicate that you spend an average of 1 hours per day watching TV or working on the computer. While some time on these activities is okay, you should try to limit the total time to less than 2 hours.

ActivityGram provides information about your normal levels of physical activity. The ActivityGram report shows what types of activity you do and how often you do them. It includes the information that you previously entered for three days during one week.

Figure 13.1 Sample ActivityGram Report.

PROVIDING FEEDBACK TO CHILDREN USING ACTIVITYGRAM

To help children learn how to interpret their ActivityGram Report, devote time during class to covering the components of the report. To help you provide valuable feedback, scan back through chapter 3, including the guidelines for children's physical activity. The following subsections of this chapter provide information to help explain the results in each category of the report.

Additional Resources

For additional information about physical activity assessment, as well as the reliability of the ActivityGram assessment, see the *FitnessGram/ActivityGram Reference Guide* (Plowman and Meredith 2013), which is available at www.cooperinstitute.org/reference-guide; in particular, refer to the chapter titled "Physical Activity Assessment" (Welk, Mahar, and Morrow 2013).

Minutes of Physical Activity

The ActivityGram Report focuses on participation in regular physical activity of moderate intensity. The Healthy Activity Zone is set at 60 minutes of activity per day; this value is higher than the typical adult recommendation of 30 minutes per day because children need to establish regular patterns of activity early in life. The higher standard also protects against the general tendency of children to overestimate their activity levels in the ActivityGram assessments. Bouts of activity that are not at the moderate or vigorous level are *not* included in the total number of minutes. Furthermore, the assessment makes no distinction between moderate and vigorous activity; this approach reinforces to children that physical activity is for everyone and that all moderate and vigorous activity is beneficial, regardless of intensity.

Time Profile

The time profile indicates the time periods when the student reports having been physically active.

Bouts of moderate and vigorous activity correspond to levels 3 and 4 on the time profile graphs in the ActivityGram Report. When interpreting the time profile, emphasize helping students identify times when they could be more active. Because the usage of time during the school day often lies beyond a student's control, the feedback for this section highlights activity patterns outside of school. For a child to be considered "active" in this section of the report, he or she must participate in at least 60 minutes of moderate or vigorous activity before, during, or after school on the reported weekdays and at least 60 minutes of moderate or vigorous activity on the reported weekend day. Feedback can be provided individually followed by a class discussion in order to help all students identify times when they could be more active.

Activity Profile

The activity profile categorizes the types of activity performed by the child based on the conceptual categories included in the Physical Activity Pyramid described by Corbin and Pangrazi (1998). Ideally, children engage in some activity at each level of the pyramid. Lifestyle activity is recommended for all students (and for adults). If students are not performing much activity, the recommendation is to begin by promoting lifestyle activity. From a health perspective, aerobic activity on the second level can correct for a lack of lifestyle activity on the first level, but it is still desirable to promote lifestyle activity among all students. It is important for students to focus on trying to do more lifestyle activity because as they become adults their time to participate in structured physical activity will be more limited and they will be more dependent on that lifestyle activity to be able to reach recommended levels of physical activity (30 minutes daily).

No distinctions are needed between the two types of aerobic activity on the second level; some children prefer aerobic activities, whereas others prefer aerobic sports. Participation in either of these categories ensures that the student is engaging in a reasonable amount of aerobic activity. Some distinction can be drawn, however, at the level of musculoskeletal activity (level 4). Specifically, students should perform some activity from both the strength and the flexibility categories; there is also likely to be some transfer between activities in the two categories.

Rest is coded at the top of the pyramid because levels of inactivity should be minimized. Feedback about this level does not mention nondiscretionary activities (e.g., class, homework, eating, sleeping). Rather, it emphasizes helping children (and parents) become aware of the child's use of discretionary time. For this reason, feedback is provided for the amount of screen time spent (watching television, playing computer games, web surfing, and using social media).

Lifestyle activities are not evaluated based on intensity. A bout of lifestyle activity is counted if it was performed for at least 10 minutes.

LIMITATIONS OF THE ACTIVITYGRAM ASSESSMENT

When interpreting ActivityGram results, acknowledge the limitations of the assessment. For one thing, it is difficult to obtain accurate information about physical activity from self-report measures for any population, and this is especially true of youth. In addition to challenges with recall, children tend to engage in sporadic activity patterns that are difficult to capture with a self-report instrument because the instrument provides a limited list of possible activities and relies on categorization of activity into discrete time intervals. Another limitation involves the fact that the results of this assessment may not generalize to the child's normal activity pattern. ActivityGram reflects only three days of activity, whereas experts agree that a monitoring period of about seven days is required in order to accurately represent normal activity habits.

Although these limitations may influence the accuracy of the test, they do not detract from its educational value. Therefore, we recommend that you acknowledge the limitations of the instrument and focus on using it for its primary function: teaching children about physical activity. Even if the results are not completely accurate, the process of reflecting on their activity habits provides children with a valuable educational experience.

INTERPRETING ACTIVITYGRAM LITE (YOUTH ACTIVITY PROFILE) RESULTS

Once students complete the quick survey in the FitnessGram software, they are presented with their personal ActivityGram Lite Report (figure 13.2). Teachers should spend time in class going over the reports and explaining the results. Scores

range from 1 to 5 in each of the questions reflecting on activity levels. The five blocks in the graph correspond with these scores, and students with only one or two blocks filled in for each graph should be considered fairly inactive. Like the ActivityGram time profile, this report helps children identify times when they could be more active—whether before, during, or after school. A copy of the online ActivityGram Report is also available in the web resource.

USING DATA FROM PHYSICAL ACTIVITY ASSESSMENTS

As with the fitness assessment, FitnessGram software produces a number of reports related to ActivityGram and ActivityGram Lite. On the individual level, the assessment and reporting process can help both the student and his or her parents become more aware of the student's levels of physical activity and inactivity. Reports containing group-level data can be used by teachers and school administrators to document activity levels, determine areas in need

Youth Activity Profile Testimonial
Spotlight on FitnessGram and ActivityGram
Shane Sperle
Physical Education Teacher
River Ridge Middle School, Wisconsin

FitnessGram has really helped the physical education world come full circle. Students from this generation now understand that a person's body does not care so much about how well he or she performs in an activity or a sport; it cares whether the person is active and moving around. The Youth Activity Profile is a great tool for highlighting this point to the students. In fact, I think that students from this generation are on the right track thanks to tools such as the Youth Activity Profile and FitnessGram. With an ambitious, enthusiastic, and organized program advisor or lead teacher in place, these resources motivate the school, the community, and, most important, the children to become and remain physically active. The Youth Activity Profile helps educators and students see proficiencies and identify areas where there is room for improvement.

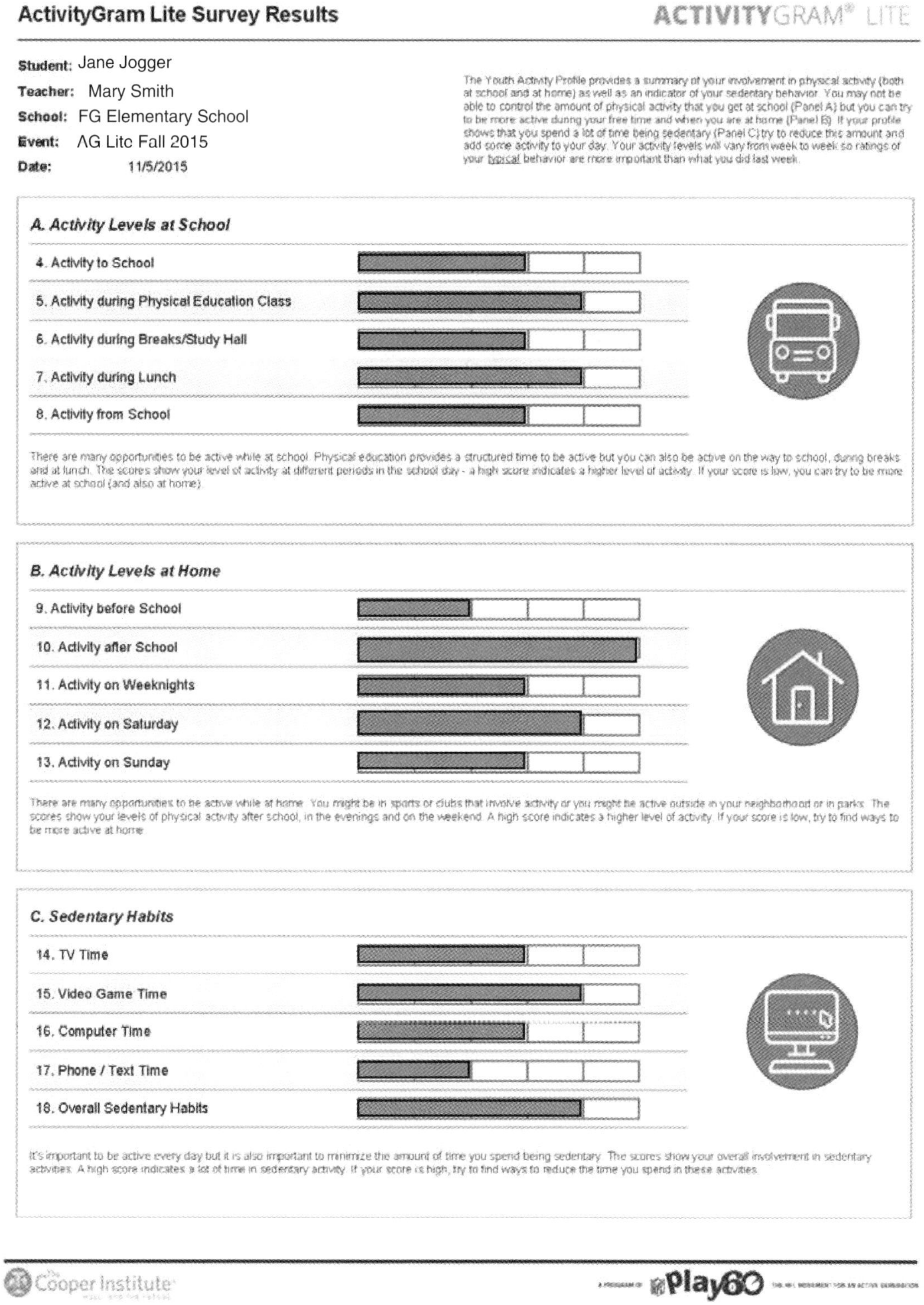

ActivityGram Lite Survey Results

ACTIVITYGRAM® LITE

Student: Jane Jogger
Teacher: Mary Smith
School: FG Elementary School
Event: AG Lite Fall 2015
Date: 11/5/2015

The Youth Activity Profile provides a summary of your involvement in physical activity (both at school and at home) as well as an indicator of your sedentary behavior. You may not be able to control the amount of physical activity that you get at school (Panel A) but you can try to be more active during your free time and when you are at home (Panel B). If your profile shows that you spend a lot of time being sedentary (Panel C) try to reduce this amount and add some activity to your day. Your activity levels will vary from week to week so ratings of your typical behavior are more important than what you did last week.

A. Activity Levels at School

4. Activity to School

5. Activity during Physical Education Class

6. Activity during Breaks/Study Hall

7. Activity during Lunch

8. Activity from School

There are many opportunities to be active while at school. Physical education provides a structured time to be active but you can also be active on the way to school, during breaks and at lunch. The scores show your level of activity at different periods in the school day - a high score indicates a higher level of activity. If your score is low, you can try to be more active at school (and also at home).

B. Activity Levels at Home

9. Activity before School

10. Activity after School

11. Activity on Weeknights

12. Activity on Saturday

13. Activity on Sunday

There are many opportunities to be active while at home. You might be in sports or clubs that involve activity or you might be active outside in your neighborhood or in parks. The scores show your levels of physical activity after school, in the evenings and on the weekend. A high score indicates a higher level of activity. If your score is low, try to find ways to be more active at home.

C. Sedentary Habits

14. TV Time

15. Video Game Time

16. Computer Time

17. Phone / Text Time

18. Overall Sedentary Habits

It's important to be active every day but it is also important to minimize the amount of time you spend being sedentary. The scores show your overall involvement in sedentary activities. A high score indicates a lot of time in sedentary activity. If your score is high, try to find ways to reduce the time you spend in these activities.

Cooper Institute

A PROGRAM OF Play60 THE NFL MOVEMENT FOR AN ACTIVE GENERATION

Figure 13.2 Sample ActivityGram Lite (Youth Activity Profile) Report.

of curricular enhancement, and identify groups of students in need of more encouragement for physical activity.

Table 13.1 describes common ActivityGram reports that can be found in the reports section in the software. It also offers an example of how each report can be used. ActivityGram reports serve as tangible reminders of students' levels of physical activity; they also provide teachers with a means for enlisting parent, faculty, and administrative support for physical education and activity programs. Teachers who do not have access to the software can distribute ActivityGram Lite (Youth Activity Profile), which is available in the web resource (figure 12.3), for each student to complete at home. However, without access to the software, it would be very difficult to develop summary and aggregate reports for the physical activity assessment.

Table 13.1 Uses of Data From Physical Activity Assessment Reports

Report	Description	Uses
ActivityGram Report	Communicates results of the ActivityGram physical activity assessment. Includes information regarding amount of activity performed, activity patterns throughout the day, and types of activity performed. Evaluates results based on the national youth guideline of 60 minutes of physical activity per day.	Students—Develop short- and long-term activity goals for academic year(s).
		Parents—Obtain information about child's activity levels and strategies to help child improve or maintain.
		Teachers—Initiate communication with students and parents; educate students about types and intensities of physical activity; educate students about recommended levels of physical activity; follow up to encourage student and parents to be active at home.
ActivityGram Statistics Report	Provides group summaries of minutes of physical activity and types of physical activity for class(es), school(s), and district(s).	Teachers—Recognize areas and types of physical activity that have improved or need improvement by individuals students or by the class; focus lesson plans according to needs of each class.
		Campus administration—Recognize which teachers have conducted activity testing and understand how many students have participated (may be used in district and grant reports).
		District administration—Track physical activity levels for district (may be used in state and grant reports).
ActivityGram Lite Report (available for students after completing the profile)	Reports results of a short survey about student's activity levels during various portions of the day (answers based on child's average week). Reports information on sedentary habits.	Students—Develop short- and long-term activity goals for academic year(s) by identifying times of the day that allow more activity time.
		Parents—Obtain information about child's activity levels and strategies to help child improve or maintain.
		Teachers—Initiate communication with students and parents; educate students about time blocks during a typical day when they can be active; teach students that opportunities for activity vary from day to day and from school to home; follow up to encourage student and parents to be active at home.
ActivityGram Lite Summary Report	Provides overview of activity profile scores at the individual level for an entire class or multiple classes.	Teachers—Recognize time blocks of physical activity that have improved or need improvement by individual students or by the class; focus lesson plans according to needs of each class.
		Campus administration—Recognize which teachers have conducted activity assessment testing and understand how many students have participated (may be used in district and grant reports).
		District administration—Track physical activity levels for district (may be used in state and grant reports).

KEY CONCEPTS

- ActivityGram provides detailed information about the amount of activity performed, activity patterns throughout the day, and the types of activity performed.

- The Healthy Activity Zone is set at 60 minutes of activity per day and makes no distinction between moderate and vigorous activity.

- Reinforce the fact that activity is for everyone and need not be vigorous in order to be beneficial.

- Be aware that children sometimes overestimate their activity time and that it can be difficult to obtain accurate information about physical activity from self-report measures. The main goals of ActivityGram and ActivityGram Lite (Youth Activity Profile) are to help students reflect on their activity habits and to provide children with a valuable educational experience.

- ActivityGram Lite (Youth Activity Profile) is a quick way to ascertain levels of physical activity for specific segments of the day and for specific locations (e.g., before, during, after school; at home), as well as levels of sedentary habits.

Bibliography

American Alliance for Health, Physical Education, Recreation, and Dance (AAHPERD). 1996. *Physical Best and children with disabilities*. Reston, VA: AAHPERD.

Biddle, S.J.W. 1986. Exercise motivation: Theory and practice. *British Journal of Physical Education* 17: 40–44.

Blair, S.N., Clark, D.G., Cureton, K.J., and Powell, K.E. 1989. Exercise and fitness in childhood: Implications for a lifetime of health. In *Perspectives in exercise science and sports medicine: Volume 2, youth exercise and sports*, ed. C.V. Gisolfi and D.R. Lamb, 401–430. Indianapolis: Benchmark.

Blair, S.N., Kohl, H.W., Gordon, N.F., and Paffenbarger, R.S. 1992. How much physical activity is good for health? *Annals and Reviews in Public Health* 13: 99–126.

Blair, S.N., Kohl, H.W., Paffenbarger, R.S., Clark, D.G., Cooper, K.H., and Gibbons, L.W. 1989. Physical fitness and all-cause mortality. *Journal of the American Medical Association* 262: 2395–2437.

Caspersen, C.J., Christenson, G.M., and Pollard, R.A. 1986. Status of 1990 physical fitness and exercise objectives—Evidence from NHIS 1985. *Public Health Report* 101: 587–592.

Centers for Disease Control and Prevention. 1997. Guidelines for school and community programs to promote lifelong physical activity among young people. *Morbidity and Mortality Weekly Report* 46 (RR-6): 1–36.

———. 2013. *Comprehensive school physical activity programs: A guide for schools*. Atlanta: U.S. Department of Health and Human Services.

Corbin, C.B. 1987. Youth fitness, exercise, and health: There is much to be done. *Research Quarterly for Exercise and Sport* 58: 308–314.

Corbin, C.B., and Le Masurier, G.C. 2014. *Fitness for life*. 6th ed. Champaign, IL: Human Kinetics.

Corbin, C.B., and Lindsey, R. 2005. *Fitness for life*. 5th ed. Champaign, IL: Human Kinetics.

Corbin, C.B., Lovejoy, P., Steingard, P., and Emerson, R. 1990. Fitness awards: Do they accomplish their intended objectives? *American Journal of Health Promotion* 4: 345–351.

Corbin, C.B., and Pangrazi, R.P. 1998. Physical Activity Pyramid rebuffs peak experience. *ACSM's Health and Fitness Journal* 2(1): 12–17.

Corbin, C.B., Welk, G.J., Corbin, W.R., and Welk, K. 2016. *Concepts of physical fitness*. 17th ed. Columbus, OH: McGraw-Hill.

Council on Physical Education for Children (COPEC). 1998. *Physical activity for children: A statement of guidelines*. Reston, VA: National Association for Sport and Physical Education.

Dale, D., and Corbin, C.B. 2000. Physical activity participation of high school graduates following exposure to conceptual or traditional physical education. *Research Quarterly for Exercise and Sport* 71(1): 61–68.

Dale, D., Corbin, C.B., and Cuddihy, T.F. 1998. Can conceptual physical education promote physically active lifestyles? *Pediatric Exercise Science* 10(2): 97–109.

Epstein, L.H., Valoski, A., Wing, R.R., and McCurly, J. 1990. Ten-year follow-up of behavioral family-based treatment for obese children. *Journal of the American Medical Association* 264: 2519–2524.

Gortmaker, S.L., Dietz, W.H., Sobol, A.H., and Wehler, C.A. 1987. Increasing pediatric obesity in the U.S. *American Journal of Diseases of Children* 1: 535–540.

Harter, S. 1978. Effectance motivation revisited. *Child Development* 21: 34–64.

Institute of Medicine. 2012. *Fitness measures and health outcomes in youth*. Washington, DC: National Academies Press. www.nap.edu/catalog.php?record_id=13483.

———. 2013. *Educating the student body: Taking physical activity and physical education to school*. Washington, DC: National Academies Press. www.nap.edu/catalog/18314.

Johnston, F.W., Hamill, D.V., and Lemeshow, S. 1972. *Skinfold thickness of children 6–11 years. Series 11, No. 120*. Washington, DC: U.S. Center for Health Statistics.

———. 1974. *Skinfold thickness of children 12–17 years. Vital Health Statistics, series 11, no. 132*. Washington, DC: National Center for Health Statistics.

Kline, G.M., Porcari, J.P., Hintermeister, R., Freedson, P.S., Ward, A., McCarron, R.F., Ross, J., and Rippe, J.M. 1987. Estimation of V\od\O$_2$max from a one-mile track walk, gender, age, and body weight. *Medicine and Science in Sports and Exercise* 19(3): 253–259.

Krahenbuhl, G.S., Skinner, J.S., and Kohrt, W.M. 1985. Developmental aspects of maximal aerobic power in children. *Exercise and Sport Sciences Reviews* 13: 303–538.

Langley-Evans, S. 2013. *Nutrition: A lifespan approach*. West Sussex, UK: Wiley-Blackwell.

Leger, L., and Lambert, J. 1982. A maximal 20-m shuttle run test to predict V\od\O$_2$max. *European Journal of Applied Physiology* 49: 1–12.

Leger, L.A., Mercier, D., Gadoury, C., and Lambert, J. 1988. The multistage 20 metre shuttle run test for aerobic fitness. *Journal of Sport Sciences* 6: 93–101.

Locke, E.A., and Lathan, G.P. 1985. The application of goal setting to sports. *Journal of Sport Psychology* 7: 205–222.

Lohman, T.G. 1987. The use of skinfold to estimate body fatness in children and youth. *Journal of Physical Education, Recreation, and Dance* 58(9): 98–102.

———. 1992. *Advances in body composition*. Champaign, IL: Human Kinetics.

Malina, R.M. 1996. Tracking of physical activity and physical fitness across the lifespan. *Research Quarterly for Exercise and Sport* 67(3): 48–57.

Massicote, D. 1990. *Project # 240-0010-88/89: Partial curl-up, push-ups, and multistage 20 meter shuttle run; National norms for 6 to 17 year-olds.* Montreal: Canadian Association for Health, Physical Education, and Recreation and Fitness and Amateur Sport Canada.

McSwegin, P.J., Plowman, S.A., Wolff, G.M., and Guttenberg, G.L. 1998. The validity of a one-mile walk test for high school age individuals. *Measurement in Physical Education and Exercise Science* 2(1): 47–63.

Morrow, J.R., Going, S.B., and Welk, G.J., eds. 2011. FITNESSGRAM: Development of criterion-referenced standards for aerobic capacity and body composition. *American Journal of Preventive Medicine* 41(4) supp. 2: S63–S144. www.cooperinstitute.org/american-journal-supplement#aerobicfitnessstandards.

Morrow Jr., J.R., Mood, D.P., Disch, J.G., and Kang, M. 2016. *Measurement and evaluation in human performance.* 5th ed. Champaign, IL: Human Kinetics.

National Association for Sport and Physical Education (NASPE). 2003. *What constitutes a quality physical education program* (Position statement). Reston, VA: NASPE.

———. 2004. *Physical education's critical role in educating the whole child and reducing childhood obesity* (Position statement). Reston, VA: NASPE.

———. 2007. *Physical education teacher evaluation tool* (Guidance document). Reston, VA: NASPE.

———. 2009. *Appropriate uses of fitness measurement* (Position statement). Reston, VA: NASPE.

Pangrazi, R.P., Corbin, C.B., and Welk, G.J. 1996. Physical activity for children and youth. *Journal of Physical Education, Recreation and Dance* 67(4): 38–43.

Pate, R.R., Baranowski, T., Dowda, M., and Trost, S.G. 1996. Tracking of physical activity in young children. *Medicine and Science in Sports and Exercise* 28(1): 92–96.

Pate, R.R., and Hohn, R.C. 1994. A contemporary mission for physical education. In *Health and fitness through physical education,* ed. R.R. Pate and R.C. Hohn, 1–8. Champaign, IL: Human Kinetics.

Pate, R.R., Ross, J.G., Dotson, C., and Gilbert, G.G. 1985. The new norms: A comparison with the 1980 AAHPERD norms. *Journal of Physical Education, Recreation, and Dance* 56(1): 28–30.

Plowman, S.A., and Meredith, M.D., eds. 2013. *FitnessGram/ActivityGram reference guide.* 4th ed. Dallas: Cooper Institute. www.cooperinstitute.org/reference-guide.

Ratey, J.J. 2008. *SPARK: The revolutionary new science of exercise and the brain.* New York: Little, Brown and Company.

Robert Wood Johnson Foundation. 2011. *The Texas Youth Fitness Study: Program results report.* www.rwjf.org/content/dam/farm/reports/program_results_reports/2011/rwjf69806.

Ross, J.G., Pate, R.R., Lohman, T.G., and Christenson, G.M. 1987. Changes in the body composition of children. *Journal of Physical Education, Recreation, and Dance* 58(9): 74–77.

Sallis, J.F., and Patrick, K. 1994. Physical activity guidelines for adolescents: Consensus statement. *Pediatric Exercise Science* 6: 302–314.

Sammann, P. 1998. *Active youth: Ideas for implementing CDC physical activity promotion guidelines.* Champaign, IL: Human Kinetics.

Schiemer, S. 1996. The pacer—A really fun run. In *Ideas for action II: More award winning approaches to physical activity.* Reston, VA: American Alliance for Health, Physical Education, Recreation, and Dance (AAHPERD).

SHAPE America. 2009. *Appropriate instructional practice guidelines, K-12: A side-by-side comparison.* Reston, VA: SHAPE America.

———. 2014. *National standards and grade-level outcomes for K-12 physical education.* Champaign, IL: Human Kinetics.

———. 2015. *Physical education program checklist* (Guidance document). Reston, VA: SHAPE America.

SHAPE America, Borsdorf, L., and Boeyink, L., eds. 2011a. *Physical Best activity guide: Elementary level.* 3rd ed. Champaign, IL: Human Kinetics.

SHAPE America, Carpenter, J., and Sinclair, C., eds. 2011b. *Physical Best activity guide: Middle and high school levels.* 3rd ed. Champaign, IL: Human Kinetics.

SHAPE America, Ayers, S., and Sariscany, M.J., eds. 2011c. *Physical education for lifelong fitness.* 3rd ed. Champaign, IL: Human Kinetics.

Slaughter, M.H., Lohman, T.G., Boileau, R.A., Horswill, C.A., Stillman, R.J., Van Loan, M.D., and Benben, D.A. 1988. Skinfold equations for estimation of body fatness in children and youth. *Human Biology* 60: 709–723.

Troiano, R.P., Berrigan, D., Dodd, K.W., Mâsse, L.C., Tilert, T., and McDowell, M. 2008. Physical activity in the United States measured by accelerometer. *Medicine and Science in Sports and Exercise* 40(1): 181–188.

Troiano, R.P., and Flegal, K.M. 1998. Overweight children and adolescents: Description, epidemiology, and demographics. *Pediatrics* 101(3): 497–504.

Troiano, R.P., Flegal, K.M., Kuczmarski, R.J., Campbell, S.M., and Johnson, C.L. 1995. Overweight prevalence and trends for children and adolescents. *Archives of Pediatric and Adolescent Medicine* 149: 1085–1091.

U.S. Department of Health and Human Services (HHS). 1996. *Physical activity and health: A report of the Surgeon General.* Atlanta: U.S. Department of Health and Human Services, Centers for Disease Control and Prevention, and National Center for Chronic Disease Prevention and Health Promotion.

———. 1998. *Clinical guidelines on the identification, evaluation and treatment of overweight and obesity in adults.* Bethesda, MD: National Institutes of Health and National Heart, Lung and Blood Institute.

———. 2008. *Physical activity guidelines for Americans.* Atlanta: U.S. Department of Health and Human Services, Centers for Disease Control and Prevention, and National Center for Chronic Disease Prevention and Health Promotion.

———. 2013. *Comprehensive school physical activity program: A guide for schools.* Atlanta: U.S. Department of Health and Human Services, Centers for Disease Control and Prevention, and National Center for Chronic Disease Prevention and Health Promotion.

———. 2014. *Youth Risk Behavior Surveillance—United States, 2013. MMWR 2014;63(SS-4).* Atlanta: U.S. Department of Health and Human Services, Centers for Disease Control and Prevention, and National Center for Chronic Disease Prevention and Health Promotion.

Welk, G.J. 1999. The youth physical activity promotion model: A conceptual bridge between theory and practice. *Quest* 51: 5–23.

———. 2012. *Youth physical activity profile.* Ames, IA: Iowa State University.

Welk, G.J., Mahar, M.T., and Morrow Jr., J.R. 2013. Physical activity assessment. In *FitnessGram/ActivityGram reference guide,* ed. S.A. Plowman and M.D. Meredith, 5-1–5-19. Dallas: The Cooper Institute.

The Wellness Impact Report. 2013. GENYOUth Foundation, National Dairy Council, American College of Sports Medicine, and American School Health Association. www.genyouthnow.org/reports/the-wellness-impact-report.

Weston, A.T., Petosa, R., and Pate, R.R. 1997. Validation of an instrument for measurement of physical activity in youth. *Medicine and Science in Sports and Exercise* 29(1): 138–143.

Whitehead, J.R., and Corbin, C.B. 1991. Youth fitness testing: The effects of percentile-based evaluative feedback on intrinsic motivation. *Research Quarterly for Exercise and Sport* 62: 225–231.

Williams, D.P., Going, S.B., Lohman, T.G., Harsha, D.W., Webber, L.S., and Bereson, G.S. 1992. Body fatness and the risk of elevated blood pressure, total cholesterol, and serum lipoprotein ratios in children and youth. *American Journal of Public Health* 82: 358–363.

Winnick, J.P., and Short, F.X. 1985. *Physical fitness testing of the disabled: Project Unique.* Champaign, IL: Human Kinetics.

———.1999a. *Brockport Physical Fitness Test manual.* Champaign, IL: Human Kinetics.

———. 1999b. *Brockport Physical Fitness training guide.* Champaign, IL: Human Kinetics.

———. 2014. *Brockport Physical Fitness Test manual.* 2nd ed. Champaign, IL: Human Kinetics.

About The Cooper Institute

The Cooper Institute is dedicated to promoting lifelong health and wellness worldwide through research and education. Founded by Kenneth H. Cooper, MD, MPH, The Cooper Institute translates the latest scientific findings into proactive solutions that improve population health. Key areas of focus are research, advocacy, adult education, and youth programs. Through these initiatives, The Cooper Institute will continue to help people lead better, longer lives now and well into the future. For more information, visit CooperInstitute.org.

You'll find other outstanding
physical education resources at

www.HumanKinetics.com

In the U.S. call 1.800.747.4457

Australia. 08 8372 0999

Canada. 1.800.465.7301

Europe . . . .+44 (0) 113 255 5665

New Zealand 0800 222 062

HUMAN KINETICS
The Information Leader in Physical Activity
P.O. Box 5076 - Champaign, IL 61825-5076